THE

Cutter's Practical Guide

TO

CUTTING AND MAKING

BRITISH LIVERY GARMENTS

Bibliografische Information der Deutschen Nationalbibliothek:
Die Deutsche Nationalbibliothek verzeichnet diese Publikation
in der Deutschen Nationalbibliografie; detaillierte bibliografische
Daten sind im Internet über www.dnb.de abrufbar.

Reprint of the original from 1895
© 2025
Republished by Sven Jungclaus
https://www.becomeatailor.com

Verlag:
BoD · Books on Demand GmbH, In de Tarpen 42,
22848 Norderstedt, bod@bod.de
Druck:
Libri Plureos GmbH, Friedensallee 273, 22763 Hamburg
ISBN: 978-3-7693-4023-5

BRITISH

LIVERY GARMENTS

IN ALL THEIR VARIETIES,

AND

COURT DRESS.

BEING

Part Four

OF

The Cutter's Practical Guide

TO THE CUTTING ALL KINDS OF GARMENTS.

BY W. D. F. VINCENT.

Author of "The Federation Prize Essay on Trouser Cutting," &c., &c.

LONDON:
PUBLISHED BY THE JOHN WILLIAMSON COMPANY LIMITED,
AT THE "TAILOR AND CUTTER" OFFICE, 93 & 94 DRURY LANE, W.C.

"W.D.F. Vincent was born in Junie 1860 and began his career as an apprentice with Frederick Cooper in Yeovil. After completing his training, he briefly established his own businesses in Oxford and later in Maidenhead as a clothier and tailor, though neither venture was financially successful.

While in Maidenhead, Vincent won an essay competition on tailoring, which was open to all members of the National Federation of Foremen Tailors, titled "The Great National Work on Trouser Cutting, or Defects in Trousers." He submitted his entry under the pseudonym "Oxonian" and won the first prize. This success led him to secure a position with The Tailor and Cutter magazine. In the early years, Vincent contributed numerous articles on tailoring methods and techniques to the magazine. However, due to the terms of his employment, these articles were published without attribution to him.

By the 1890s, Vincent became a leading tailoring authority. His books, such as The Cutter's Practical Guide to the Cutting & Making of All Kinds of Trousers, became standard reference work. By 1917, Vincent referred to himself as a journalist. He died in June 1926.

The Tailor and Cutter magazine and academy were operated by John Williamson & Co Ltd. In the 1950s and 1960s, many tailors displayed their Tailor & Cutter Academy Diplomas, signed by W.D.F. Vincent, as the Chairman of Examiners, as a centerpiece in their shop windows. One such example can still be seen on display at the Museum of Welsh Life at St. Fagans in South Wales."

(cf. https://vincents.org.uk/family-history/w-d-f-vincent-tailor; 15.12.2024)

This edition is a reprint of the legendary *Cutter's Practical Guide* series; the first book was published in 1890. Although W. D. F. Vincent wrote many books on tailoring, these are the most popular. The entire text has been meticulously read, and the images have been carefully cleaned and edited to ensure the highest quality.

Content

PREVIOUSLY PRINTED BY THE JOHN WILLIAMSON COMPANY LIMITED,
93 & 94 DRURY LANE, LONDON, W.C.

https://www.becomeatailor.com

AUTHOR'S PREFACE

The Work we have now completed, and which will be placed before the members of an intelligent profession, is in a large manner the outcome of practical experience in high-class livery trade. But as the experience of one on so wide a topic as all kinds of Liveries must of necessity be of a limited nature, we have gladly availed ourselves of a large circle of trade friends, many of whom are engaged in some of the most noted Livery trades in this great City of London. Many of these have materially helped in the preparation of this Work, for which we extend to them our hearty thanks, feeling assured that the ideas and hints gained from such sources have such a practical bearing on the subject of Liveries, that the value of the Work has been largely enhanced thereby. We have spared neither trouble nor pains to make this work as complete as possible, and trust it will supply a felt want in tailoring establishments.

W. D. F. VINCENT.

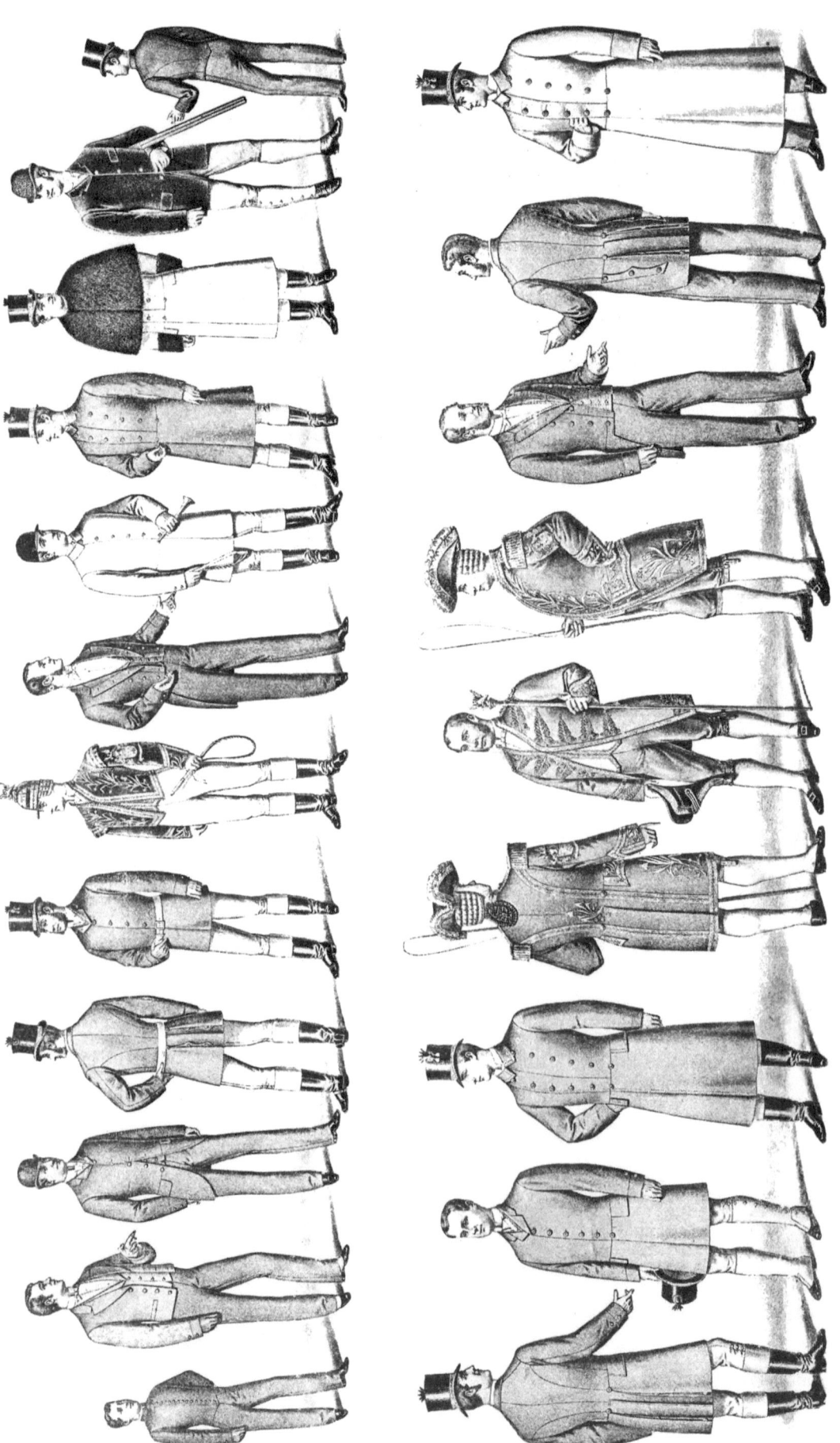

BRITISH LIVERIES.

ILLUSTRATING THE GARMENTS THE SYSTEMS OF WHICH FORM THIS WORK.

This is an uncoloured Miniature of the New Plate just published at the "Tailor and Cutter" office, details of which will be found on another page.

THE
CUTTER'S PRACTICAL GUIDE
TO
LIVERY GARMENTS, &c.

INTRODUCTION.

In treating of Livery Garments, it will be well if, at the start, we get a correct definition of what livery is. The dictionary explains it as follows: —

"LIVERY. — That which is delivered out stately, as clothing, food, etc., especially the peculiar dress by which the servants of a household are distinguished; peculiar dress appropriated by any body of persons to their own use; company of those wearing such a garb; any characteristic dress or outward appearance; an allowance stately given out; *v.t.*, to clothe in livery."

Liveries are of very ancient origin. When the ancient Greeks used that pithy saying, "The dress shows the man", they intended it to convey that it proclaimed his social condition, quite as much as his moral character. The custom of livery is really derived from the term *liberata* or *liberatio*, a term applied to the delivery or distribution (made by the Merovingian and Carlovingian races) of particular sets of clothes to the servants throughout the palace, and at the sovereign's expense. In common phrase this was called a *livrée*, and it was ordinarily performed in the plenary courts of France. We also find a term of similar signification used by the early German emperors.

In the days of chivalry, livery, in the proper sense of the word, often covered noble backs; the duke's son was page to the prince, and wore his livery. The earl's second son serving a duke donned his master's coat and colours. The knight's second son, and the esquire's son, joyfully wore the livery of him they served, whilst many cases are recorded of the younger brothers of noblemen serving their elder brother, and wearing with all humility their elder kinsman's coat and badge.

The badge on the arm is distinctly traceable as far back as Edward IV, and consists of a cloth or metal circle, worn on the left arm, and displaying the crest of the wearer's master. This is only retained by the few at the present time, such as the fraternity of Watermen, who wear the "Doggett's coat and badge," the Lord Mayor's servants (illustrations of which are given on our Livery Plate), as well as here and there a company of firemen, &c. This mode was at one time so general, that when people desired to apply a proverb to people lacking the ordinary appendages, they said, "like a coat without a badge." The badge was probably peculiar to England, as it appears to have excited the curiosity of foreigners in the time of Queen Elizabeth. Laced cloaks were given as livery in the time of James I. For a considerable time livery was worn by other common men, besides salaried servants; they were looked upon as the retainers of him whose livery they wore, and their service was that of the strong hand, which was ever ready to be raised in their master's services. So formidable a body did they become in time, that the law at last stepped in, and decided that without license no noble could retain such followers; and permitted the master to give livery only to his own household servants, officers, and counsel learned in the law. When this law was evaded, as it sometimes was, the penalty of imprisonment was enforced, and increased by fine of £5 per month for every retainer kept without license. The Earl of Oxford, at Hemingham, on one occasion received a visit from Henry VII, and in order to do him honour, had a large muster of retainers specially for this occasion. The king, after thanking him for his good cheer and hospitality, said: "I may not endure to have my laws broken in my sight. My attorney must speak with you." The poor Earl was mulcted in the enormous sum of £10,000, for merely putting livery on the back of a few score men, contrary to the statute of Henry's first Parliament.

Queen Mary signed thirty-nine licenses in her five years reign, whilst her sister Elizabeth signed only fifteen in thirteen years; the former Queen gave permission to Bishop Gardiner to maintain two hundred livery servants, whilst Elizabeth only allowed her Archbishop (Parker) to keep forty, and to no one did she grant permission to keep more than one hundred.

Licences and retainers were both abolished in the reign of Charles II, and since that period livery has only been worn by the lower class of household servants.

Many of the livery appendages may be traced to fashion once patronized by nobles. The old style of long waistcoat, a few years ago so generally worn by the groom, is the old undercoat of the squire, and the three cornered hat of the coachman once figured at sovereign courts on aristocratic brows.

At one time the French liveries were of the most gorgeous description, but the fashion and the word so betokened a menial, that liveries were abolished by the Constituent National Assembly as incompatible with a republican system, founded on the tripod of liberty, equality and fraternity.

Many instances are on record of livery servants making an immense fortune by speculation, in such schemes as the South Sea and Mississippi, and after having amassed these fortunes, and setting up carriage, horses and livery servants of their own, so far forgetting themselves as to take their old seat on the box. Baron Ward is a good example of a man beginning as a livery servant and rising to eventually become at the close of his career Prime Minister to the late Duke of Parma.

Livery is a term that has often been used by the poets. One puts "April's livery" on spring; Milton speaks of twilight as the "silver livery" of the evening; Hood described the livery of the earth as "grass green turned up with brown," &c.

"Livery" is a term also applied to the ninety-one companies of the City of London, the members of which formerly wore clothes resembling in both form and colour those of the Lord Mayor and Sheriffs. Of these companies, the "Merchant Taylors" occupies the position of seventh. It possesses large property, and a noble hall where they feast and make merry. The first twelve of these companies were at one time known as "honorable", they are now merely known as "great". On next page we give the coat of arms of the "Merchant Taylors", which, in addition to the connection it has with livery, will doubtless interest our readers generally.

From this introduction to liveries from a historical and general standpoint, we will proceed to treat of them more directly, practically, and so in harmony with the object of our treatise. We will proceed to note a few of the

Special Features of Livery Garments.

Speaking generally, they should be made without any attempt to follow the prevailing fashion. Plainness, neatness and service-

CONCORDIA PARVÆ CRESCUNT

ability must be the ideals aimed at. The edges are invariably finished bluff, except when piped with another colour cloth; or, in the case of livery overcoats, which, owing to the thickness of the material used, are more often finished raw edge, and double stitched. This remark does not, of course, apply to full dress livery, where the most elaborate braiding and trimming is used. The linings are always of the plainest description; the sleeve lining, for instance, should be a self colour, such as slate or light drab; stripes being in all cases conspicuous by their absence. The body lining too (except in the case of full dress livery garments and for the page boy) should be free from stitching or any-

thing of an ornamental nature, all wadding and padding being secured by merely flash baisting.

The workmanship must be such as will stand hard wear; the buttons must be sewn on well, the pockets firmly stayed and tacked, and made generally with a view to hard wear, rather than for appearance. With all this they must be neat, and the fit must be above reproach, for livery servants are generally very smart men, who are most particular about their appearance; and being continually in the presence of their employers, are naturally desirous of appearing at their best; so that any approach to clumsiness in make, fit, or finish would be a serious defect in a livery garment. Livery servants require, and indeed will have, consideration; so that, whilst regulations must be adhered to, yet their own pet ideas and notions must not be ignored. The best guide we know of for liveries, is an old garment of the same kind, as worn by the same servant; it being a noted fact that families employing liveried servants are generally very conservative, seldom changing the colour, style or finish. Fashion's hand — although distinctly discernible, as in the old style of notched collar end now being obsolete — touches liveries very lightly, and the changes are almost imperceptible in this respect; so that liveries may, to all intent and purposes, be regarded as being unaffected by fashion.

The materials used for livery garments are generally of a heavier and somewhat coarser make than used for gents' garments, as for instance, the difference between a refine and a superfine.

The Rules for the Selection of Colours

Are as follows. First in importance, consult your customers' wishes. If they ask your advice, then recommend that the coat be of the same colour as the body of the carriage is painted, with a fine piping the same colour as the fine lines on the carriage; the buttons the same colour as the harness fittings; and the vest, if of striped Valencia, the same as the band on the horse's forehead. For the overcoat, advise either a drab Devon or a Devon of the same colour as the lining of the carriage. These are the recognized rules for the tailor's guidance, but inasmuch as families have their fancies in this respect, they are not adhered to in all cases.

Buttons are a somewhat important feature in liveries. They are mostly made from a specially cut die, which costs in the first place from 30s. to 40s., and which is charged to the customer; but this only applies if he has not had buttons of that particular die before, as once the die is cut it lasts for all time. The tailor having taken the order, writes to his button makers, and gives the name of the family and description of the button; or, better still, an old button. They will then make them or get them made; this takes some days, so that it is advisable to order them as soon as possible, as one cannot get on far with the majority of livery garments without the buttons, a large number of them being plugged; indeed, all that are used for ornament only are put on thus, which consists of making a hole in the cloth with the bodkin, and forcing the shank through it, and fastening it on the other side with a plug of linen or canvas.

Messrs. J. Platt & Co. have a special arrangement for the supply of dies for livery buttons. They offer to make them at half the usual cost, provided the die remains their property; and in this way brings them all orders for this particular make of button.

Buttons can be ordered from stock with plain or fancy letters, called initial buttons; and in addition to these there are the plain doctors' buttons, used largely by those who do not care to go to the expense of crested buttons, such people, for instance, as only keep one servant.

The number of buttons required for the various garments are as follows: Overcoats, 18 large; Coachman's Frock, 12 large, 4 small; Coachman's Vest, 8 small; Footman's Coatee, 22 large, 4 small; Footman's Vest, 4 or 5 small; Groom's Frock, 12 large, 4 small; Page's Jacket, 16 or 18 ball buttons. Full dress garments vary according to the style of trimming. Crest buttons are used on dress livery breeches, but on all others the ordinary breeches buttons are used; ordinary buttons are also used for gaiters.

In the event of mourning, the crest buttons are generally changed to plain black flexible, and if the garments are not made from black, then cloth bands are put on the arm, as well as cuffs and collar of the same colour. These bands are generally put on the left arm just above the elbow, about two inches wide. Some firms put the band on the right arm for the coachman, and on the left arm for the footman, so that it may look symmetrical when they are seated on the box.

As the tailor often has to supply the silk hat, it may not be out of place to say that the cockade, if there is one, is placed on the left side. There are various patterns of cockades, full particulars of which can be obtained from most hatters' price lists. The cockade is put on by the aid of a hairpin and a cork. First find the position desired (the fan part of the cockade should come above the crown); then two holes are made in the side of the hat, and the hairpin put through cockade and hat, and fastened over a cork on the inside. Livery silk hats are heavier than the ordinary style, and are made more with the view of exposure to bad weather than the ordinary

kind, so that when ordering it should be stated they are for livery. Hats sometimes have silver lace binding and band, in which case the bow of the band comes in the front.

It is impossible to lay down any definite rules as to

When Livery is Supplied.

Each family makes its own regulation in that respect, but it will be well for a record to be kept, so that the servants may be advised when their livery is due. As a general rule, all servants have two suits a year and an overcoat every other year, though this latter garment is sometimes only supplied when wanted. Coachmen and grooms are supplied with stable clothes, and footmen with pantry jackets, the frequency with which these are supplied depending largely on the amount of wear given them; probably one plain suit per annum would be enough, with two Dress suits; drawers or pants are always supplied with each pair of trousers or breeches that are unlined.

With some servants, such as for instance the huntsman, two suits are supplied at once, as he being exposed a good deal to all sorts of weather, it is necessary he should have a dry suit ready for the next day, if he comes home at night wet through. Being closely connected with this aspect of liveries, we feel we ought to refer to the custom of the trade with regard to a delicate question, viz., the almost universal habit servants have of "making" a suit now and again; that is, by care and judicious management they are able to keep their last suit without wearing it, or at any rate worn so little that a press up will make it as good as new. He then brings it to the tailor, who forthwith examines it and forms his judgement as to whether it is good enough to

pass muster; if he is satisfied on this score, he presses it up and does what he thinks necessary, and then sends it home as a new suit; and enters it in his ledger accordingly, the servant having the option of either having the amount in other ordinary goods or of having a cheque for the amount.

Many have been the disputes, and not a few law suits, between employers and tailors, on this point, when such practices have been discovered; the employer sometimes going the length of charging his tailor with dishonesty, whilst the latter has pleaded that inasmuch as the clothes were supplied to the man as part of his wages it could make no difference to the employer, as well as stating that it was the custom of the trade. The tailor is helpless in the matter, for were he to refuse to comply with these requests, he might soon anticipate losing the majority of his livery trade, as servants have a great deal of power in this respect, and we know many employers who ask if the last suit was satisfactory, previous to giving orders for the next, and it is on these and similar occasions that servants are able to do the tailor a good or bad turn, according to the state of the relations existing between them. Many has been the half sovereign we have known to pass between tailor and servant, with the view of either bringing fresh trade, or keeping the old, when it has been somewhat shaky.

It may not be out of place if we look at this question from all sides, and we can only repeat that it is

Much to be regretted

Such an unsatisfactory state of things is necessary to carry on a successful business; as the tailor runs many risks of losing his customer if it is found out, as well as reducing his legitimate profits by allowing the servant more than the proper garments

would have cost him to produce. Looking at it from the servant's point of view — it may be viewed from many standpoints — and the following is the one which perhaps relieves any qualms of conscience be may have on the matter. He is engaged by his employer at a fixed salary, and so many suits per annum, board, lodging, &c., and he looks upon his clothes in the light of part of the payment he receives for his services, and if he can by care save perhaps one out of every three suits, he considers he is quite at liberty to do what he likes with it. Looking at it from this standpoint it may not be regarded as dishonesty, as he has as much right to be careful over his clothing as he is over his money. We refer to this as it is a point on which many tailors have had grave doubts, but cannot see their way clear to avoid it; and although it is the pretty general custom of the trade, yet the practice should be avoided as far as possible, as viewing the matter as an abstract principle, it certainly has the appearance of a want of straightforwardness between the tailor and his customer, and the sooner this system is altered, and one introduced recognized by the servant's master, the better will it be for the status of the tailoring trade.

We will now proceed to deal with the various garments used in livery.

Additional information

Please also note the excerpt from the Daily Mirror newspaper on page 83.

LIVERY TROUSERS.
Plate 1.

There are two kinds of Livery Trousers: the ordinary walking trousers used by footmen, and the open cut style used by the coachman and groom. The measures necessary are 1 length of leg; 2 length of side; 3 size of waist, 4 size of seat; 5 size of knee, and 6 size of bottom desired. In addition to these the undress thigh taken closely at the fork will be very advantageous in dealing with customers with large or small thighs.

Diagram 1

Illustrates the mode of applying these measures in the production of the draft. Unroll the cloth and see that the way of the wool runs from right to left, or so that it will run down the trousers. Line O O is the selvage edge of the cloth; mark up from O to B say 1½ inches, or rather more than the amount of the turn desired; from B to C the leg length, and B to A the side length. From C to E is ⅙ seat, and B to O is ¼ of the size of bottom, plus 1 seam (¼ inch); from O draw a line to E, and from this square across to C and to D and F; from E to D is $\frac{1}{12}$ seat, and D to F is $\frac{1}{12}$ seat plus ¼ inch (or if the thigh measure is preferred, ⅛ of the tight undress thigh, plus half the difference between the two thighs, usually 1½ inches, thus: ⅛ of 21 = 2⅝ ÷ half of 1½ = 3⅜. Square up from D to H by line D C, and shape the fork by a graceful curve starting it about ⅙ seat above D, and making the hollowest part opposite D ¼ inch more than half D F. G is at the hollowest part of the waist, and from G to J is ¼ waist plus 2 seams; from H to I the top is squared across by line H D. I is sprung out a little from J, and from J to K is rounded in the style illustrated on diagram, making K, which should be the most prominent part of the side,

one-twelfth seat above C. K is rounded in the style illustrated on diagram, making K, which should be the most prominent part of the side, $\frac{1}{12}$ seat above C.

We now come to the distribution of width of the leg, and the first thing is to locate the position of knee, which is got by coming down from E to L the half leg measure, minus 2 inches. From L to M and L to N are both ¼ knee width, with one seam added, and from O to P is half an inch less than O B. Measure up the length of leg from F to P, and complete the topside as per draft. In cutting, leave sufficient on at bottom below P and B to form the turn up, certainly not less than 1 inch. If side pockets are ordered, then leave a pocket facing on the topside from J to K, which would be about 6½ inches, as it makes a much thinner pocket mouth.

The Undersides. Diagram 1.

These are cut by placing the cut out topside down on the cloth in position most convenient; and as nothing is required in this system beyond F, that point may be brought close up to the edge of the material. From D to Q is $\frac{1}{12}$ seat, but as this fixes the amount of stooping and bending capacity, this may be increased for very easy trousers; but it must always be remembered ease is produced at the expense of appearance. The more seat angle there is given from D to Q, the more surplus length there will be in the seat when the wearer is standing up. Draw a line from Q to C, and draw seat seam Q S R at right angles to it; and then continue seat seam from Q to F by the same curve as the topsides. Now proceed to measure up the seat, making Q to K and S to U the half seat measure, plus 2 inches. This 2 inches is allowed for the four seams consumed in making, and one for ease, and to allow for the expansion of the body (which is usually 2 inches) when sitting. From G to J, and R to T, measure up the waist measure and 2½ inches, which amount allows for a 1 inch fish being taken out at A. This fish should not be V shaped, but smaller at the top as illustrated. It should terminate a full ⅛ of the seat above line C D, and should run rather backward. This fish facilitates the fit in many ways; it makes the hips smart fitting at the sides, locates the surplus width just where wanted, and provides ease on the top edge of the trouser, for the increased size of the body above the waist. To get the seat piece, make N a pivot and sweep from I to T; put the square on the seat seam, and square across from R to T, come in from R to V 2 inches and go up 1½. Complete the sideseam from T through U N to B; if a very close thigh is desired the curve from U to B just opposite C may be reduced. Measure the size of bottom from B to P and B to W the size of the bottom, plus 1 inch, and complete the undersides as per dot and dash line.

It only now remains to put in the balance marks, and take out the dress, and the trousers are complete. In taking out the dress, come back from F to X the amount desired, usually 1 or 1¼ inches, taking care that X is so far from M as F is, and then hollowing gradually from just below G, taking out nearly as much at Q as there is from F to X. An inlay should be left down the sideseams from T to B of say 1 inch; the same amount down seat seam from R to F, and occasionally an inlay at F of about ¾ inch, running in to nothing, about 7 or 8 inches down is useful. See that the balance marks are *snipped*, as marks easily rub out, and it is very important, especially with livery trousers with a piping down the side, that the sideseam should not be twisted. The best way of securing that is to see the balance marks are kept level. (See Appendix for instruction how to pipe the sideseam of trousers.)

Coachman's Riding Trousers.
Diagram 2.

The full instructions for working out the system for these will be found in the Appendix, it being placed there in order to allow the remaining diagrams to face the pages of type treating of them.

BREECHES. Plate 2.

On this Plate we have the two principal types of Livery Breeches, and from the description of the principle on which these are based, any kind of breeches may be cut. They are of two distinct kinds — the close and the open style; so that what would be looked upon as a virtue for the one kind would be a fault in the other.

Footman's Dress Breeches.
Diagram 3.

These are made long enough to just clip over the knee, say 3 or 3½ inches below the knee, so as to come to the smallest part. An extra ½ inch of length is left on the topsides to full on over the knee, to facilitate the bending of the leg. They are cut on the same method as the Dress Trousers illustrated on diagram 1, the width of the leg being distributed on either side of centre line at L I O, though the topside may be cut about ½ inch narrower at N and B, and this amount made up at Y Z, so that in the case of the knee being 14, from L to M would be 3¾, which equals ¼ knee, plus 1 seam. L to N would be 3¼, or ½ inch less than former quantity, and in order to compensate for this, L to Y would be 4¼.

These Breeches are made from plush and have this peculiarity, viz., that the topsides are made with the pile to run down and the undersides up. They are usually made up with whole falls at the top.

The knees are finished with three buttons of the regular livery crest, and the bottom band of the knee is trimmed with a silver or gold lace garter and below this hangs down a little tab known as a "cock's comb".

The Breeches should fit very clean and smart about the fork, so that dress should be taken out. The size about the upper parts of the thighs need not be too close.

Silk stockings and patent leather shoes with plated or silver buckle is worn with these.

In making garments from plush, it is necessary to baste a piece of paper on the one part, otherwise it "creeps" when sewing the seams. The diagram will illustrate the other details, so that we need only say that the usual 2 inches is allowed over the seat and 2½ at the waist; and a fish of 1 inch taken out as shown.

Coachman's Breeches. Diagram 4.

These garments will come to the ordinary cutter fifty times to the former kind once, hence they are of more importance. These are cut open in the style of to cut, the distance from 9 to ? being not less than 1 inch, whilst the same amount is added to the seat angle beyond the $\frac{1}{12}$ of seat, when measuring from D to Q, and the topside lowered at H 1 inch.

The measures required are, fork to knee, to small, to calf to bottom, sideseam top to knee, size of waist, seat, knee, small, calf, and bottom, the four latter being preferably taken on the bare leg, and taken closely. In addition to these measures, the measure of thigh at fork and the mid-thigh measure may be taken. The system is as follows: —

A to C, difference between side to knee and leg to knee measures. C to E $\frac{1}{6}$ seat; E to D $\frac{1}{12}$ seat; D to F $\frac{1}{12}$ seat, plus ¼ inch, or $\frac{1}{8}$ tight thigh, plus ¾ inch; D H and E squared at right angles to C F;

E to * $\frac{1}{12}$ seat; E to 9, 9 inches; 9 to ? the amount it is desired to open the legs, generally 1 inch for this class of breeches; E to L on line drawn from * through 9; the length of leg from fork to knee, plus 1 inch; from E to I fork to small, plus 1 inch; and on to O ; fork to calf, also plus 1 inch; square lines at right angles to this line from these points, and mark off the widths of leg as follows: On the legseam as from L to M ¼ of the tight leg measures taken over calf, small, or knee, plus 1 seam (¼ inch) and from L to N, 1 inch less. G J is ¼ waist, plus 2 seams, and Q K is ¼ seat.

To cut the undersides, fold the topsides over the extra inch of length given to the legs, and proceed to to run the legseam by the topside. Find the seat seam by coming up from D to Q $\frac{1}{12}$ seat plus 1 inch. and squaring by Q C to R. Come out from N 1 inch and sweep from A to T, and mark 1 inch above as illustrated, and find top of seat piece as explained for trousers. Measure up waist, allowing 2½ inches, and seat from Q to K, and S to N, the half seat and 2 inches. Make up the size of the knee from N to M, and M to Y to knee, plus 1 inch, treating the small and calf in the same way. If thought advisable, apply the mid thigh measure about point 9, and allow 1 inch for making. This is a very useful measure, as it is very important to make coachman's breeches *tight* fitting in the legs, and close fitting in the seat.

The material from which they are mostly made is white buckskin, though drab kersey is also often used. Making has much to do with the success of this garment, and those of our readers who desire it will find some hints on making in the appendix at the end of the book, as well as full description of Diagrams 5 and 6.

The same principle as above described applies to all Breeches. Gents' loose baggy Breeches are cut by opening the legs

1½ inches, increasing the seat angle 1½, and allowing 3½ or more over the seat, the distribution of width being done in the same way, only they are made very loose-fitting from fork to knee.

CONTINUATIONS, LEGGINGS, AND GAITERS.
Continuations. Diagram 7. Plate 3.

Both Livery and Gents' Breeches are often continued below the calf, sometimes as far as the ankle, the idea being that Breeches are worn with stockings and Continuations with half-hose. These Continuations are mostly made from a thin material similar in colour to the Breeches, such as white Flannel with Buckskin or drab Melton with drab Kersey. The method of cutting these is as follows: A B straight line; A to C half calf plus seams; B D half bottom plus seams; A B is the length; C D is the seam which goes up the back of the leg. These are cut without seams at leg, it being far preferable to have the seam up the back of the leg where the prominence of the calf exists. From A to G and A to E are both ¾ of an inch less than O B of Breeches, Diagrams 3 and 4; H B being the same amount; E to I and F to J are both 1 inch or sufficient to form a button-stand.

Gamekeeper's Leggings. Diagram 8.

These leggings are made to fit the leg closely all the way down, so that they have to be hollowed a fair amount over the foot to get it to lie fairly smooth at that part. The system for cutting these also forms the foundation for cutting the other styles, and is as follows: Draw line A B, and mark off the length desired plus seams, if the material will not stand raw edge; A to C is the distance from the top to the calf, usually 2 or 3 inches; C to B divide into three equal parts, as at D E, and from these points square line across and mark off half the size of the leg at these respective stations, plus seams. As a general rule D H is 1 inch less than C G, and E I is 2 inches less. Add on ⅜ of an inch of round at J as shown and reduce the top at F in the same way. Hollow over the foot from B to U 1½ to 2 inches. To find the position of the buttons, take the Breeches and put the calf to the calf line, and place the centre line of the Breeches ¾ of an inch outside the front line of leggings, as illustrated from L to C; K L is the centre line of Breeches, A C, is the centre line of Leggings. Now mark at O the position of the buttons, and as these buttons are kept straight down the side, make O A and P B equal; the edge at S and T is about 1 inch beyond the line O P, so providing for a button stand. Q is as far from A as O is, which also applies to R, being as far from U as P is. The usual number of buttons is seven, but this can hardly be looked upon as a regulation number. In making, these Leggings are generally lined through and the back seam stitched on either side to keep the lining firm.

Livery Leggings. Diagram 9.

This is a style of Legging that is largely patronized for Grooms, &c. They are made to imitate Gaiters as far as possible, and although bearing a resemblance to gent's leggings they are yet quite distinct from them. The back part behind line A B is the same as Diagram 8; the chief difference is the extra size at bottom from J to U, which is made half width of bottom desired, plus seam, and the centre line gradually sprung out from C through D. The same method of adjusting the position of the buttons is followed as before described, though in this case the buttons are more forward. The centre line being hollow, these will require an amount of manipulation, such as stretching the edge of the button-hole side just above R, and shrinking it on the centre line in the same way as for trousers. In making, these are finished in a very similar style to the Gamekeeper's, though they are sometimes left unlined, the button hole edge being faced with the same material. A tab is sewn on, or else a slit left at the top of the calf seam to allow them being fastened to the calf button of breeches. The usual number of buttons is 7, though sometimes 8 are placed as arranged on Diagram 10.

Livery Gaiters. Diagram 10.

The part behind A B is the same as for Diagram 8, though they are sometimes left fuller between G and J; a little looseness at H I being looked upon as a virtue by some coachmen; in any case they should not fit too close. From J to U measures half the size of bottom desired, and draw line from U to E, E being one seam in front of line A B. The buttons of Livery Gaiters always run towards the heel, which feature is fully illustrated. Q is as far from A as O is, and R is as far from centre line D B as T is. The half tongue is illustrated by dot and dash line P F E, and round by solid line U B and P. These Gaiters consist of three parts: the half tongue, E, T, P, B, U; the topsides, Q, F, J, U, R; and the small half, O, F, J, P, plus the button stand. Gaiter straps are placed as shown, not less than 3½ inches from J, the buckle being placed on the inside of foot. These leggings are generally faced all over the tongue part, and a facing put up the button hole side, and if left raw edge a narrow strip is put round the top to take the stitching. The seams over calf and tongue are stitched on either side to keep them firm. The regulation number of buttons is eight — seven marked at equal distances apart,

and then one placed between the two top ones. The kind of buttons generally used are pearl gaiter buttons. The material mostly used is either drab Devon or Kersey, though we have made them from Whipcord.

COACHMEN'S VESTS.
Plate 4.

Vests are by no means an unimportant feature in Liveries, and although the fancy styles of long skirted Vests, &c., are now a thing of the past, yet a considerable amount of character is often introduced to a Livery suit by the colour and finish of a Livery Vest. The material from which they are made varies; sometimes it is the same as the coat, with edges, &c., finished in the same way, or it may be a self-coloured Cassimere of bright colour, such as red, or it may be a striped Valencia, in which latter case the colour in general harmonizes with the forehead band of the horse's trappings. The stripes of a Coachman's Vest runs vertically, or in other words lengthways on the figure, whilst those for a Footman runs horizontally, or round the figure. Grooms' are made as a Coachman's.

Coachmen's Vests are generally made very long, say 27 or 28, finished over the hips with a slit at the side-seam; they button high, and for dress — that is ordinary dress with the Frock Coat — it is made with a roll collar as illustrated on Diagram 13, the opening of coat and vest being so arranged that the Vest shows just a piping above the crease edge of coat, whilst for stable wear and ordinary purposes, they have the choice of either the no-collar or step collar finish at neck.

The System. Diagram 11.

We will not here describe the method of taking the measures; but our readers will find full particulars of that in the Appendix.

Sufficient here to say, the only special measures required are from nape to opening — not the top button, but where the opening actually comes, and on to the full length. These in addition to the ordinary measures taken for the coat will suffice, and are applied in this way: Square lines O 2½, O 17, and mark off O to 9 the depth of scye. O to 17 the natural waist, and from these points square off at right angles; come in from 17 to 1, 1 inch, and from 1, come in ¾ and shape back seam as shown, curving the waist in to point ½ where it joins the line from 1 to O; from O to 2½ is $\frac{1}{12}$ of the full breast, minus ½ inch; from ½ to 9¾ is one-fourth breast, plus ¾ inch; from ¾ to 8¾ is one-fourth of the waist, plus ¾ inch; now make a pivot of ½ and sweep from O to W; shape the back neck by coming up from 2½, ¾ inch, and from this point measure off ⅛ breast, plus ½ inch; from these points complete the back, shaping the back scye as illustrated, and giving a little spring below the waist line at both back and sides; the length of the back has to be got from the forepart.

The Forepart. Diagram 12.

Drawline O C O 10½, and make from O to 8 the same distance as 9 17 of the back; take out 1 inch from 8 to 1 for all sizes, large and small, and shape under arm seam. From O to 9¾ is ¼ breast plus ¾ of an inch, and from 1 to 8¾ is ¼ of waist plus ¾; from 9¾ come back to 2¼ the across chest measure minus ½ an inch; this finds the front of scye, and from these two points we locate the front shoulder. To find point F, take the front shoulder measure, minus ¼ inch on account of its being a Vest, and deduct the distance O ¾ of back from it; and by the remainder sweep as indicated by dotted line 12¼ in the direction of F. Let us give an example

of the working of this: Suppose the front shoulder to be 12½; deduct ¼ inch for its being a Vest; that leaves it 12¼. Now deduct distance O ¾, which we will say is 2¾, and that will leave 9½, which is the amount by which to sweep or describe part of a circle from pivot 2¼ to find point F. Now add ¾ of an inch to this, and sweep again in the same manner from point 9¾, and where these sweeps cross each other locates the neck point F. To find point D we take the over shoulder measure and first deduct ¼ inch on account of it being a Vest, and then deduct the distance from ½ to W of the back as illustrated by dotted line ½ 9, and then by the remainder sweep by putting the tape on 2¼, and then putting the finger on the tape 1½ inches up and sweeping for D. Suppose the over shoulder to be 17; deduct ¼, leaves 16¾; deduct ½, 9, which is 9 inches, leaves 7¾, which is the amount used. From F to D is ¼ inch narrower than the back, and by these points shape the scye; from F to V is $\frac{1}{12}$ breast minus ½ an inch, and from this point draft through 9¾ and 8¾ to find the breast line. Now apply the length, deducting O ¾ of back, and measuring from F to A the opening, and from F to B in a straight line the full length plus seams; ¾ is sufficient for this, though many allow 1 inch and do not find it too much. The shape over the hips is a matter of taste, but if a guide is desired, come down from V the same distance as F V, and making that a pivot sweep from B to C, and shorten C about ½ inch above sweep. If there is to be a collar, shape gorge as diagram 13; if no collar, full in the gorge ¾ of an inch as illustrated on Diagram 12. Complete the draft by adding on a button-stand of ¾ of an inch on both button and hole side, and if thought desirable to leave on an extra wide button stand on the button side that may be done to taste.

The last Plate illustrated more particularly the system, and the only point we need further mention on this head is, that the system works the same for corpulency as for the normal figure; the only little difference is in the back, where, for a very corpulent figure — and there are corpulent coachmen now and then — come in from 17 to 1, ½ an inch only, and from 1 to ¾, ¼ inch only.

The no collar vest illustrated on Diagram 12 is only used for stable wear, or, in other words, it does not find a place in either Dress, or Full Dress Livery, but it is nevertheless a very popular style for stable wear.

The roll collar style illustrated on Diagram 13 is the most general style, and is always used for Dress wear, whether the Vest is made from the same material as the coat, a bright coloured Cassimere or a striped Valencia. They are always made to fasten close up to the neck, and arranged to just show a piping above the crease row of the turn of coat. There are usually eight Livery crest buttons. When made from Valencia, the stripes always run vertically as illustrated on Diagram 13. The back for the Valencia Vest would be of a light colour, and the lining plain, as striped linings are not the thing for Liveries as we have already noted.

Sleeve Vest. Diagram 14.

On this Diagram we illustrate the Sleeve Vest, a garment that frequently causes the cutter considerable trouble. It is a far more difficult garment to cut than a coat, for the sleeve problem asserts itself here in full force. A Sleeved Vest is required close fitting, and yet to have plenty of room for easy movement, and as the arms are moved in every direction in wear, it is evident the sleeve must not have a suspicion of drag anywhere. The scye must fit close up to armpit, as the Vest being worn fastened and so held tight to the waist, there is no possibility of its being lifted away from the sides when the arms are raised, as is the case with coats too deep in the scye. Whilst this is very important, it must not be carried to an extreme to produce discomfort. It will be noticed the back is wider, the shoulder being made ⅙ breast from ¾ past W to the end of shoulder — or if preferred, the width of back may be applied direct, plus seams. The across chest measure is only reduced ¼ inch instead of ½ as for an ordinary Vest, the object being to get the scye to fit as close as possible without being tight.

The general finish of this Vest and the details of the system are the same as described for Diagrams 11 and 12. The back and forepart being drafted separately, they are merely placed together in this draft so that we may describe the sleeve system easier. This Diagram illustrates the step roll collar, the outline at I showing how the gorge is cut, though some firms cut the gorge down to 1 inch above the turning point of roll, and make both collar and step of some thin material, such as Silesia. It does not necessarily follow that Sleeve Vests are always made with step roll collars; we merely illustrate that mode of finishing the neck on this Diagram, so that all kinds may be shown in the series. Sleeve Vests are as often made no collar or roll collar as they are with step collar for Livery, as both Dress and Stable Vests are made with sleeves. When cut long, as Coachmen's Sleeve Vests usually are, they are often left with a slit at the sides as shown by the stitching on this Diagram; it gives freedom for the hips.

The Sleeve. Diagram 15.

The system for sleeve is as follows: Place back and forepart together, as illustrated on Diagram 14, so that the depth of scye line forms a continuous straight line. Now square up from this line to the most backward part of the back, as illustrated by dotted line between ½ and 10¼, and measure the distance between that line and point 11¾ of the forepart. Now (coming to Diagram 15) draw lines at right angles as O 4½, O 5, and mark off from O to 5 the distance got from the scye. Next mark the pitches of sleeve, the forearm ¾ of an inch up from a level of the scye at 11¾, and the back pitch one-ninth of the half breast down from the shoulder point of back. Now place the back in a closing position at the shoulder, and measure the distance across from back pitch to front pitch straight. Come down from O to 1 of sleeve 1 inch and apply the distance between the pitches from 1 to 9; O to 4½ is half this quantity, and by these points the sleeve head may be drawn. Now mark off the length of the sleeve to elbow and cuff, allowing for the three seams consumed from sleeve head and back; hollow the forearm 2 inches at elbow, and mark off the width to taste — ⅙ breast plus 1 inch is a very good guide, the width of cuff being ⅛ breast plus ¾; these are merely guides, and the customer's taste should be considered. For the run of cuff sweep from the top of hindarm, point 9 on line 1. For the underside, measure *round* the bottom of the scye between the two pitches, and apply this measure from 5 to 7¼ and shape the under sleeve as shown, with a little round rather than hollow.

The sleeve lining is usually sewn in with the seam of the outside in dressmaker fashion. The cuff is finished with one hole and button; a brace button is used for this.

In cutting Sleeve-Vests, the points to give special attention to are: 1st. Get the scye as close up to the arm as possible. 2nd. Give plenty of width to the sleeve head; err on the side of too much rather than too little. 3rd. Never hollow the under sleeve at the top. For fuller details of the sleeve system see explanation of Plate 16.

FOOTMEN'S DRESS VESTS.
Plate 6.

On this Plate we illustrate the Dress Vests worn by the Footman. In small families, Full Dress is seldom supplied, so that the Dress Vest for them is the style illustrated on Diagram 17, which may either be of striped Valencia of the same pattern and colour as the Coachman's, illustrated on Diagram 13, or it may be the same colour as the Coat, or a bright coloured Cassimere. Of course the Coachmen's and Footmen's Vests would be made from the same material, otherwise there would be a want of harmony between them when seated on the box. There is this difference, however, between them: when the Vest is made of striped Valencia, the stripes run round the figure as illustrated on Diagram 17 for the Footman. The Footman's vest is much shorter than the Coachman's; it should be made to harmonize with the strap of the Coatee, though sometimes they are made to just show a piping below the strap. The usual number of buttons is four, and the style of opening as illustrated on Diagram 17. As will be seen, the mode of cutting is the same as was followed for Gent's Dress Vests before the introduction of the horseshoe style of front. The gorge is cut from F through 9¾, the bottom of the gorge being terminated about 2 inches above the point it is intended to turn; the remainder of the roll is formed by the collar as shown on Diagram 19.

Full or State Dress.

In large families the State or Full Dress Livery is a very important feature, and is even more worn by them than the Morning Dress as illustrated on Diagram 17; indeed, so much is this so that it is customary for them to have two sets — a State Dress and a semi-State Dress. The latter would probably be made from cloth elaborately trimmed, whilst the former would be made from Velvet, Satin, or light Cassimere, not only elaborately trimmed with lace, but also extensively embroidered with gold.

Diagram 16 is a reproduction of a State Dress Vest made for a recent Lord Mayor of London. The material was white Cassimere laced on the edge with gold lace to match the coats, and embroidered in the bottom corner with gold in the form of a spray. There were two welt pockets placed in the ordinary position with the welts trimmed with lace to match the edges. On the occasions above referred to there was a semi-State Dress Vest, which was made from blue Refine to match a coat of the same material; this was also edged with lace and gold Russia braid, but the last was not of so elaborate a character as in the former.

As regards the cutting of these Vests, they are cut as a no-collar Vest at the neck, but as they are only intended to hook and eye they are merely cut to come to the breast line. This Vest is longer than usual and the bottom corner of the front is cut rather sharply away. In the olden time these Vests were arranged with skirts and pointed flaps and worn very long, but that has been relegated to the styles of the past, and the only indication that such styles ever existed lies in the fact that they are now cut extra long and the corners cut away.

Details of Making.

In making up garments to fasten with hook and eye, they should be arranged so that there is one hook and one eye alternately all down each front; the eye should be allowed to come beyond the edge, but the hook should be rather further from the edge than the eye is over; because it is sure to "draw" a little; both should be securely fastened to the canvas. The effect when finished, should be two edges just meeting and not showing any gap; nor, on the other hand, should the edge ridge up.

BUCKLE AND STRAP. — This should be placed just in the hollow of waist, and preferably carried into the sideseam and tacked through back a couple of inches from the seam. If the Vest is a washing one, the buckle should be fastened by aid of a linen button and button hole. Some livery servants prefer tapes to the back of their Vests, in which case there should be two

POSITION OF POCKETS. — The welt, pockets should be put as nearly as possible in the hollow of waist, a trifle higher or lower if the Vest is long or short. In Dress Vests when flaps of an ornamental character are used, the opening to the pocket mouth is at the top of the flap, not underneath. Welts generally run 5 inches long and about ¾ inch wide; they are placed nearer the sideseam than the forepart; sometimes they are carried in to the sideseam, but this is only suitable when the forepart is narrow. Watch pockets are generally 3½ inches wide, and the welt ⅝ deep; it is arranged in the slant, and about in the position shown on Diagram 14.

The Collar System. Diagrams 18 & 19.

Mark point 1 the front of turn or ¼ inch above the top hole; come up from 2 to 3 the stand of collar desired, minus ¼ inch. Draw line from 1 through 3 to 4; come down from 4 to 5 the difference between the stand and the fall, and draw crease row from 5 through 3 to 1.

From 5 to 6 the depth of stand, and 5 to 7 the width of fall; point 8 is a matter of taste, and must be done in harmony with lapel. The length of collar at 6 is got by a trifle more than the width of back neck from shoulder of forepart. Let collar overlap forepart at 9 about ¼ inch, and complete as diagram, letting there be a little hollow at 5, and rather more spring from 5 to 7 than from 5 to 6. Diagram 18 shows the ordinary stand and fall step collar for Vests or Coats, whilst Diagram 19 illustrates the roll collar used for various garments, such as Vest, Diagram 17. Gent's Dress Coats, Dressing Gowns, &c., the principle being the same, though the outline 9 would be a little different.

THE COACHMAN'S FROCK.
Dia. 20. Plate 7.

We now come to deal with the Livery Coats; we have taken the Coachman's Frock first, as it is the garment most frequently required. Its special features are: Single-breasted Frock, buttoning rather high, with six plated buttons, a rather full skirt, long side edges in the back pleats extending the full length of skirt, with three buttons arranged, one at the top, one about one inch from the bottom, and the centre one a trifle, say ½ an inch nearer the top than the bottom one. Pockets on the hips with flaps cut to follow the skirts about 9½ inches long and 3½ deep; the pockets should be arranged to run rather forward than otherwise. The scye is cut forward, and the sleeve made to hang forward in accordance with the position of the arm when on the box, driving. This position must also be remembered when making, and the sidebody well strained down when sewing it to the forepart at the sideseam; if this is not done, there is sure to be a quantity of superfluous length when the wearer is seated. It is well to let them sit down in a chair when trying them one, so that the true position in which they will be worn may be attained.

The style of cuff mostly used is illustrated on Diagram 21; the stitching, seam, or piping that forms the cuff is placed 2 inches up from the bottom of cuff, and one hole and button placed above and one below it, as there illustrated.

The System.

This being the first coat, it is necessary we explain the system. Draw lines O, 19, O, 2½; O to 3½ is ⅓ depth of scye plus ½ inch or to taste; variations here do not affect the fit but merely the style, any alteration being adjusted by the front. O to 9 is the depth of scye, O to 17 the natural waist, to 19 fashion waist, and continue to bottom full length, plus 2 seams. Draw lines at right angles to all these points, and make O to 2½, ¹⁄₁₂ breast, minus ½ inch; about 2 inches below 3½ apply the across back measure plus 2 seams, and slightly curve it out to shoulder point. From 17 come in 1 inch and draw back seam, continuing below 17 at right angles to 1. From ½ to 20½ is the half chest measure, plus 2 to 2½ inches; this allowance is varied according to the degree of tightness the measure is taken, the thickness of the material, and the desired amount of ease. For a fairly taken measure and a smart fit from a refine cloth. 2 inches will be enough, that is, measuring from ½ *not* 9. From 20½ come back to 12¾ a trifle less than the across chest measure; the reason for a trifle less is the advanced position of the arms when driving. From 12¾ make a sweep; take the front shoulder measure, and deduct the width of back neck O, ¾, and the remainder sweep for F, using 12¾ as the pivot, now add 1 inch to the quantity thus used, and make point 20½ the pivot, and make another

sweep as indicated by dotted lines 13½. Where these two segments intersect each other, locates the neck point F. Now measure from ½ to W, deduct that from the over shoulder, and by the remainder sweep from point 12¾ as indicated by D, putting the finger on the tape 1 inch above 12¾ before sweeping. Make the width of the front shoulder ¼ inch narrower than the back, and shape the scye as shown, making it as hollow as possible at 12¾ — certainly not more than ¾ of an inch away from the angle, letting it touch a line drawn at right angles from 12¾ at 1½ inches up and 1½ inches back from 12¾; keep the back scye just at the top of the sidebody as close up as possible, and let the top of the sidebody come a good ¼ inch in advance of the back. We next locate

The position of the Seams.

The width of back at scye is $\frac{1}{18}$ breast, which is also the width of the back at waist; a line is drawn from 17 to the top of sideseam, and point 4½ is ¾ inch in from this line, and the back sideseam is drawn as illustrated. Take out 1½ to 1¾ inches from 3 to 4½, and draught the sidebody seam as shown, taking out fully ¼ inch at top. The length of the sidebody is got by sweeping from the bottom of back sideseam just opposite 19, making a pivot of the top of sideseam.

From this point draw a line at right angle to O 19, to find the run of the waist seam. The underarm seam is got by squaring down from 9½ which is ¼ breast from ½ and taking out 1 inch at waist, ½ inch on either side of line as shown at 9 10. Now measure up the waist, and allow 2½ inches over the waist measure as illustrated. The run of waist seam is got by hollowing it 1 inch at side. The gorge is got by coming down from point V the same distance as F V, and the forepart is completed by adding on a button stand of 1¼ inches all through.

The Skirt System.

Come down from A to S 2½ to 3 inches and draw a line from S to hip button, and from there at right angles down 9 inches and up 1, and draw line from hip button through this point, add on ½ inch of round and the back of the skirt is done; now come ¾ inch above line from S to hip button, just below the under arm seam, and shape top of skirt by the points so obtained. From hip button come down to * the same distance as A S; put one arm of the square at *, and let the angle rest at A and get run of front at right angles to * A. Now mark off the length by deducting the length of back to fashion waist, applying that to hip button, and continuing to bottom of skirt the full length desired, plus 1 inch. Make length of front same as at back, and draw bottom of skirt from these points.

FOOTMAN'S COATEE.
Diagram 22. Plate 8.

From the Coachman we come to his companion on the box, the Footman. His coat for Morning Dress or what is known as Dress in small families, is termed a Coatee, and is in style the same as a gent's Dress Coat, with several important variations, of which the following are the chief; Cut shorter in the skirt, the usual length being 2 inches above the bend of the knee, and this gives the skirt a much heavier appearance; there is a long side edge extending the full length of pleat with three buttons as described for the Coachman. In the centre of the skirt a sword flap is put on about 11 inches long and 2 inches wide at the points, a reference to diagram will show the shape as well as the position of this, though it must also be noticed that many firms take the top of the sword flap up into the waistseam. This sword flap is really nothing more

than a piece of cloth seamed on the skirt down the front (straight) side in the desired position and turned over and either stitched or piped down the top, back and bottom. Three buttons are placed on this, and as they are for ornament only they are plugged — that is a hole is made with a bodkin, and the shank of the button forced through, and a plug of canvas or linen put through the shank at the back and sewn on either side. The lapel is cut rather heavier than a Gent's Dress Coat — say 1¾ at bottom, 3 at the widest part, and 2½ at top. It is made with two holes above the turn and 3 below. Whenever possible the lapel should be cut on the crease as illustrated in the lay Plate. This makes a far nicer edge, and prevents any possibility of dissatisfaction on account of ravelling raw edges. Twenty-two large buttons are used for the Coatee; 4 on each breast, 3 on each sword flap, 3 on each side pleat, and 2 for a link. In addition to this the cuff has 4 buttons as usual, and arranged in the same way as described for the Coachman, and illustrated on Diagram 21.

The System

For producing the body part is the same as explained for the Coachman, with the exception that the across chest is made the full width taken on customer. The same amount is allowed over the chest measure, viz., 2 inches when measuring from ½ to 20½, but in measuring up the waist, only 1 inch is allowed over the waist measure, as this garment is never worn buttoned, only fastened together at the top with links as illustrated on Diagram 22. The gorge is lowered fully 1 inch below dotted line, and the run of line V to 20½ is purely a matter of taste, so that whether more is added on or some taken off between those two points, it will only affect the width of lapel.

The skirt system is somewhat different from the coachman's: the line is drawn in this instance at right angles from the line drawn across from bottom of sideseam to bottom of forepart; from this come down 9 inches and go out, 1 inch, and draw line from hip button through this, and add on ½ inch of round. Come up ¾ inch above line at top just below the under armseam, and take out a good ½ inch in front. The width of the strap in front would be cut 1¾ in front and 2 inches at back, and the length one-third of the entire width of the skirt at the top. The width of the bottom is 1 inch more than half the distance of the top, and the run of the front of skirt slightly rounded, and the bottom run up slightly towards the front.

The cutting of the sleeve is fully described in the description of Plate 16, so that we need only note that the Footman requires a fairly forward-hanging sleeve, as his arms are being continually brought forward when in the act of waiting at table.

Details of Finish.

The skirt is always lined through with cloth, and the pockets are now more generally put in the pleat. The breast facing should be good and brought to the bottom of the strap. The sewing to edge of the lapel is cut straight or, only the least bit hollowed, and should be rather shorter than the forepart, and skirt so that it can be put on slightly tight opposite the round of the breast. When the edges are piped, the edging goes round the collar and collar ends, down the lapels along the strap and down the front of the skirt, but not along the bottom. It goes up the back to the tack and also along the top, back, and bottom of the sword flap, but not down the front. A row goes round the cuff 2 inches from the bottom as described for the Coachman.

Occasionally collars of different colour cloth, finished with snipped or notched ends, and trimmed with a fancy design of worsted lace, but these are relics of the olden times which are rapidly dying out.

The links are generally made by fastening two Livery buttons by the aid of a split ring which method is much neater than fastening them together with a bar of thread as well as taking far less time.

GROOM'S FROCK.
Plate 9.

The Groom's Frock partakes very much of the same character as the Coachman's, but as the Groom is generally a smaller man, or as is often the case, a lad, the fronts are much shorter, so that the number of buttons up the front is sometimes reduced to five, the tailor using his discretion in this matter. The length of the skirt is also very much reduced, as this garment is only made to come well over the seat, a skirt of 10 or 11 inches is quite long. Occasionally we see Grooms with Frocks as long as a Coachman's with flaps and pockets on the hips, but this is out of the usual order of things, and may be looked upon as the exception. The rule respecting Groom's Coats, is that there shall be no flaps on the hips, and that the pockets shall be placed at the pleats, whether they are in or out pleat, is a matter of taste. The side edge is made short, the regulation length being 9 inches for the Groom, and either pointed as Diagram, or else the back edge straight and pointed down at the bottom, three buttons being placed on as usual. A ticket pocket is generally placed in the seam and frequently an in breast pocket is added.

The Cutting

Of these garments needs one or two points of explanation. What we have previously described, as regards the system for the Coachman's Frock, we will take as a basis, and the first point that requires our notice is: that being worn with a leather belt as they generally are, the waist requires to be cut much closer than ordinarily, or otherwise ridges of material will appear under the belt. It will be noticed on referring to Diagram 23, that an extra ½ inch is taken out at the underarm seam, and if an extra quarter inch is taken out between 3 and 4½ of back and sidebody, it would not do any harm, as the coat is drawn close to the hollow of the body, and so will allow of this extra suppression. In measuring up the waist, only allow one inch for making up beyond the actual waist measure between the back seam and the breast line, beyond which the usual 1¼ inches of button stand is allowed. The skirt is got by dropping down 2½ in front before squaring down to 9 to find the pleats, but this is just as described for the Coachman. It must be remembered in cutting for Grooms, they are smart, natty little men, and will not tolerate anything of a clumsy character in their dress; so that the cutter must be able to produce a garment smart in fit and finish, if he would please them.

The Making.

If the edges of this garment are piped, the piping would go round the collar, down each front, up the back skirt, and across the sleeves — just the same indeed as the Coachman's, only that there being no flaps on the hips they cannot be piped.

The skirt is often lined with lining of the same colour as the Breeches, which are not unfrequently of white Buckskin, in which case the lining would be white; but there is no universal rule in this respect, so the cutter must use his own judgment. In making the side edge it will be necessary to turn in the pointed part and line it, plugging the buttons through in the ordinary way. The edges are bluffed in the usual way, and, as previously stated, a seamed and opened edge is the best for these garments; when it is turned in and felled it is apt to get ragged and rough after a little wear. Some experienced cutters always direct their workmen to put the stay tape down the right forepart in a line with the buttons and not on the edge as usual, contending that by this means a cleaner-fitting forepart is secured when the buttons are fastened, and doubtless this would be so. The other usual stretchings and shrinkings or drawing in should be done as for an ordinary coat, and as our readers are conversant with them we will not again repeat here, but proceed to notice the other articles of

Groom's Dress.

He usually wears Breeches, either of drab Kersey or white Buckskin, though we have made them from Tweed. They are made close-fitting in the style illustrated on Diagram 4. Top boots, leggings, and gaiters are all worn with these. The gaiters are illustrated on Diagram 10, and the leggings on Diagram 9, and as full instructions are given on the page treating of these we need not again repeat here.

The Groom's Vest is cut in the same style as the Coachman's illustrated on Diagram 13, and if from Valencia the stripes run the same way as the Coachman's, viz., vertically. The Overcoat is made up without flaps on the hips, has a 12 inch side edge, with skirts reaching to just cover the knee, and in all other respects as the Coachman's, though the ticket pocket would be in the waist seam.

A Groom's Stable Suit might either be made in the Lounge or Morning Coat style. Diagrams of both styles appear on another page. As a general rule, the Groom himself has power to decide the style of his Stable Dress, though the tailor must carefully avoid any tendency to the extreme of fashion.

Grooms seldom or ever wear Full Dress Livery; their special care is the horses, and do not find a place on the box where Full Dress is worn.

BUTLERS' DRESS COAT.
Plate 10.

The Butler occupies a very different position in the household to any of the other servants, he being practically the chief of those whose work lies indoors, and, as might naturally be supposed, his garments are made in a different style. There is very little about a Butler's clothes to indicate they are Livery, for they approach more nearly the Gent's Dress Suit than any. Livery buttons are never used, plain flexible buttons taking their place. The cloth of the coat is black Superfine, and we have known them made from a fine dress Twill, but this is quite the exception, the black Superfine being the correct thing. There are none of those ornaments, such as sword flaps, side edges, &c., used on this coat; indeed, it is a plain Dress Coat as worn by gentlemen, the edges finished in the usual style, and on no occasion piped or trimmed in similar ways. The style of cuff most used is the ordinary gent's cuff, formed about 3½ inches deep, and finished with two holes and buttons, the buttons being black flexible as on the body. The fronts are generally made with two holes below the turn and 3 in turn, and the lapel made lighter and smarter than for the Footman.

The Cutting. — Diagram 24.

There are several points to notice in cutting this garment, the principle of which is the same as for a Gent's Dress Coat.

The Butler's duty is to rule, or in other words to undertake the management of the servants beneath him; and as this is not a very laborious office, but rather one requiring the exercise of mental rather than muscular qualities, his garments may be made much closer fitting. Starting with the back first, it may be cut ¼ inch narrower across the back pitch, and a quarter inch narrower all down, so that the width of back at waist would only be 1¾ inches for a 36 chest. The amount allowed over and above the chest measure from centre of back to breast line should only be 1½, or at most 1¾ inches, and the shoulder produced in the ordinary way. The sideseam is carried further towards the centre of back, it being placed at one-fourth breast from construction line; but this being a matter of taste it may be made less if desired. In measuring up the waist, the combined widths of back, sidebody, and forepart from 1 to 19½ are made up to the *nett* waist measure.

The Fronts and Lapel.

In forming the gorge at I, it is lowered a good inch from the standard sweep from F by V, and from the part where the crease row crosses to I should be straight. It must always be borne in mind that the part illustrated beyond the crease row at I, is composed purely of style, and be made wider or narrower without in any way affecting the fit. The length of the forepart should be arranged in harmony with the length of Vest, a point that should not be lightly overlooked, and of course when measuring this, the width of the strap of the skirt must be remembered. The Diagram sufficiently illustrates the skirt; the strap is made one-third of the width at top, and the bottom, as illustrated by 6½ is 1 inch less than half the width at top. The skirt is generally much longer than the

Coatee, even more so in this respect than our Diagram indicates, 36 being a very usual length for a 19 fashion waist. The lapel is cut by drawing a straight line as illustrated by dots, and coming in from that ¾ of an inch as illustrated on the Diagram, and so producing a hollow sewing-to-edge. The width at bottom would be 1½ and at top about 2, the middle being made about 2¾. The top of the lapel is made fairly pointed upwards, and in making, the holes in the turn are made to run with this as illustrated on diagram. The lapel comes to the bottom of the strap, but in marking off the length it will be necessary to cut it a little — say ½ inch shorter than the forepart and strap of skirt. Although we have compared the Butler's Dress Coat to a Gent's Evening Dress, it must not be inferred that Silk facings are ever used, for there the line is drawn. His suit should be a plain fitting Evening Dress, without ornament of any kind whatever, avoiding alike the side edges and sword flaps of the Coatee, and the Silk facings or corded edges of the gent's Dress Coat.

The Butler's Vest is a plain, low-turning roll collar of the style illustrated on Diagram 17, made from the same cloth as the coat, and although some attempts are occasionally made to make the crease row hollow, yet the present style of horseshoe front, as worn by gents, is looked upon as too extreme for even the Butler's Livery.

The Trousers are made quite plain, close-fitting, and of medium width. All ornamentation in the form of piping, &c., down the sideseam, being carefully avoided. The Diagram to use for these is Diagram 1, and the material used is generally Doeskin — black of course.

This Suit is admirably illustrated on our Livery Plate, a miniature of which is placed at the commencement of this volume. The large Plate is got up in the very best style and beautifully coloured, and as it illustrates all the leading styles of Livery Garments, it should find a place in every respectable tailor's shop.

PAGES' JACKET.
Diagram 1. Plate 11.

The Page Boy is one of the smartest of all servants, and his Jacket is one that allows more scope to the tailor than any other in the respect of trimmings, &c. Page's Jackets are generally interlined with wadding, and quilted right through, the pattern of the quilting being a matter of taste, the more general being straight lines. The Page's Jacket is a short close-fitting garment, cut to extend about 3½ inches below the waist, and terminating back and front with a point. The back is cut on the crease, and consequently should be made narrower than the usual run of body coats, 1¼ inches being quite sufficient. On first looking at the diagram, some may imagine that because the back seam is drawn 1 inch in from the construction line at the waist, it cannot be taken out on the crease; but a little reflection will prove to them that any straight line can be placed on the crease edge, and the back is drawn quite straight. There is hardly so much taken out at the underarm seam as usual, because the waist is extra large, it being the usual thing in boys to find them slightly disproportionate at that part, and the rule as regards disproportion is to fill up the fish under the arm to the extent of one-sixth of the disproportion, taking a waist four inches smaller than chest as our ideal of proportion, so that in the diagram before us, there is 2 inches of disproportion, ⅙ of which is a trifle over ¼ inch, and consequently there is only ¾ inch taken out under the arm, instead of 1 inch. The neck is finished with a stand collar, so that care should be taken to avoid cutting the neck too large; the collar would be made about 1¼ inches deep. The fronts are finished in various ways, but the style illustrated is the most general, which is plain buttons and holes. The buttons are round ball shape, from 14 to 16 being the usual number. In arranging for these, only ¾ inch of button stand should be allowed on the button hole side, and 1¼ or 1½ on the button side; this is important, so that the buttons may show down the centre of the front. These Jackets are very frequently finished with studs and hooks and eyes up the front, and if this plan is followed, it will be necessary to use care in putting in the studs. The way to fasten them is "plugging", and they should be arranged to come quite close together; but there is a danger in doing this of getting them too close, when they would appear "bobbly" and so spoil the effect. Sometimes there are three rows of studs, one up the centre, and one over each shoulder, the shoulders being finished with shoulder cords fastening over a button at neck. A notched hole finished with a button is another detail sometimes added, but these fancy items are the exception rather than the rule. The cuffs are finished in many styles, the most general being as illustrated on Diagram 21; though when the edges are piped, a pointed cuff is used, the point being about 3 inches from the bottom, and ½ inch nearer the forearm seam than the hindarm, at the seams the cuff would be 2 inches deep. When the edges are piped, the piping goes all round collar, front edge and bottom edge. One inside breast pocket is generally put in on the right side, with the mouth running vertically instead of across as usually done for other coats; the necessity for this variation will be at once apparent when it is remembered the fronts have to be unbuttoned to get at the pocket.

In cutting Trousers for Page Boys, care should be taken to cut them close and smart fitting in the seat, as it must be remembered the seat is exposed to full view.

Another point in connection with the Trousers is to advise cross rather than side pockets, as it would look quite out of place to see the Page Boy with his hands in his pockets. When the edges of the Jackets are piped, the Trousers have a piping down the sideseam to correspond.

Postilion's Jacket. Diagram 26.

This Diagram illustrates the feature of this Jacket, so that a very little explanation will suffice. The back is cut on the crease and the seam under the arm is very often omitted. It fastens up to the neck either with holes and buttons as illustrated on the Pages' Jacket, or with hook and eyes and studs. It is cut to come to the waist only, and is finished at the bottom with a waist band 2 inches wide. The collar, cuffs and band are sometimes made of different colour, indeed, this garment is generally finished in a fancy style. Some put lace on all the seams and edges, whilst others confine it to the edges only. Others pipe or cord the seams, so that our readers will see that there is full scope for trimming of an ornamental character in these Jackets. Our illustration is reproduced from a photograph taken of a recent Lord Mayor's Postilion's Full Dress Jackets. The sham Vest inserted in this case was done because the man was rather stout, and is unusual. The rosette at the back is only worn for Full Dress, which remark also applies to the wig.

The Breeches are made close-fitting, and a shield is worn on the inside leg to protect it from the horse.

The Cap has a peak in front in the style shown on illustration.

HUNTSMAN'S FROCK COAT.
Diagram 27. Plate 12.

As will be seen from this Diagram, the Huntsman wears a single-breasted Frock Coat, buttoning 5, with rather long and somewhat full skirts; the length generally comes to about the knee. The cuffs are finished ith two holes and buttons, as shown on Diagram 26. It is lined through with woollen Plaid in the body, and the skirts are faced all through with either the same cloth or one of a slightly thinner make of the same colour. The material used is the same as for gentlemen, *i.e.*, either black Melton or scarlet cloth, though the Duke of Beaufort's Huntsman wears a coat made of green Plush. There is generally some distinction between the Huntsman's Coat and those worn by ordinary gentlemen: for instance, Baron Rothschild's Huntsman has a coat of black Melton in every respect as ordinary, but with a row of gold lace added to the outside edge of the collar.

These garments are sometimes made with a Prussian collar, but the more general style is the collar and turn as shown. A tab is put on the collar on the left side made to turn round so that it can be made to fasten over a button on the right collar, or turn back and be fastened on the inside of the left collar free of the crease row.

The Cutting

Of this coat demands a little special attention. In the first place it should have more allowed for making up; 2½ or even 3 inches over the half chest measure will not be too much to allow between the centre seam of back and the breast line. A little extra size in the over shoulder measure is also an advantage. The skirt should be full, and for this purpose come down 3 inches from the waist to find the construction line of skirt, and when getting the run of the front come down the same distance at the back from the hip button. It will be noticed the back is made somewhat heavier than usual, the back being cut 2¾ at waist, which is quite in keeping with the coat generally. The sleeve should be cut long and forward hanging, and it is the custom with some firms who do a big business in Hunting Frocks, to carry the forearm seam well under, adding, say, 1½ inches to the top-side sleeve at forearm and taking it off the under; and in making up, this is lapped and double stitched, the object being to avoid a seam which might act as a gutter for the rain to run through. The under sleeve should only be slightly hollowed. The sleeves are made up with wind cuffs or sleevelets. These are made about 5 or 6 inches long, and are cut the same size as the sleeves at bottom from the same material as the sleeve lining, which is usually the same as the body lining of the coat; this is fastened to the sleeve, and a piece of elastic put round the bottom to prevent the wind and rain blowing up the open sleeve. The sleeve lining is stitched round the sleeve head to the facing or seam so as to keep it from getting clumsy.

The Pockets

Are a very important feature in a Hunting Coat. Pockets are placed in the pleat, and are usually capped with Macintosh. Large skirt pockets are put in each skirt with a mouth of about 12 inches wide, fastening up with two buttons; these generally come a little below the waistseam and are always lined with Macintosh throughout. In addition to these there is an outside and an inside breast pocket and a ticket pocket, which is generally put in the waist seam and has a flap to go in or out. These pockets should be well stayed, and proper attention paid to the Macintosh covering, which material can be procured from any wholesale trimming house.

Details of Make.

A ring or button, preferably the former, is put at the back neck point by the hanger to fasten the hat guard to. A saddle strap is put at the back tack, this is a piece of cloth sewn inside the coat at the back to prevent the rain coming on to the saddle when the pleats open. In shape it is something like a patch pocket, only wider at the bottom; it should be about 8 inches deep and about the same width at the bottom, though it may be made a little narrower at the top. It must not be sewn lower down than 1 inch from the top so as to be free. Some work a hole in the bottom of this to fasten it to the saddle, but this has many objections, so that it is generally preferred plain.

The edges of these garments, whether made from black or scarlet, are left raw and single stitched; this, however, is sometimes objected to on account of the white edge the scarlet cloth shows, in which case the edge would be made up in the ordinary way, and either stitched by machine or prick stitched.

In sewing on the metal buttons with a shank, it is advisable to sew through an extra piece of cloth on the surface, or a black mark will be made from the shank of the button, the cloth can then be cut away after the button is on. The buttons used are generally metal, either Livery crest, or fancy metal button specially made for this purpose.

Fine pipeclay on a piece of lemon will remove any ordinary soil that may be made in the course of making up.

As previously noted, these garments are frequently supplied two at a time on account of their exposure to the weather.

GAMEKEEPER'S COAT.
Plate 13.

This garment bears the same relation to the gent's Shooting Coat, that the Huntsman's Coat does to the gent's Frock. It is a garment cut for a special purpose, and should be cut and made accordingly. The material — Velveteen, from which they are invariably made, is not of the pliable or workable kind, so that also must be borne in mind in the cutting. It is the common practice with some cutters to cut an ordinary Morning Coat a size or two too large, but although this may pass muster, yet it is hardly what is wanted; for although it is quite true that the garment should be easy fitting all over, yet the Gamekeeper's occupation demands extra size in certain parts only. In the first place there should be plenty of room in the front shoulder, for these men require plenty of ease in the scye, and their shoulders are generally pretty well developed. There should also be plenty of room from centre of back to front of scye; the climbing of hedges and ditches, and the bringing the arms forward, when in the act of shooting, also demands extra length of the sleeve, as well as a forward balance, or, to put it in other words — a longer hindarm.

Diagram 29

Illustrates the cutting, and as will be gathered from this, the Gamekeeper's Coat is a S.B. body coat, cut very full to the measures, with enlarged shoulders, extra size allowed for making up; a straight cut front really large enough to button easily all the way down, and a forward cut skirt with plenty of drapery at the sides. It will be noticed in the first place that the scye in this garment is deeper than most of the former ones. This is done more because the Gamekeeper has large shoulders, then because a deep scye is necessary; indeed, a scye too deep for the requirements of the figure would be one of the very worst features there could be in a coat of this class, as in that case all the weight of the coat would rest on the muscles of the arm when it was lifted as in the act of shooting. To obviate this, it is necessary to avoid hollowing out the under part of the sleeve too much; indeed, it is better not to hollow it out at all, but just take it across

straight from forearm to hindarm, and leave the extra material there for ease.

The next point to be noticed is, that we only come in ½ an inch at the waist. This is done because it is not required to get these garments to cling as close into the waist as an ordinary body coat.

The back is made full width across the back pitch, and both the back scye and the back at natural waist are increased ½ inch, so that the width at that part is one-ninth of half breast, plus ½ inch. The usual 1½ inches is taken out between back and sidebody up to nothing at 4¾; and for a proportionate figure of 4 inches smaller at waist than chest, 1 inch is taken out under the arm as from 9½ to 10½; but this is filled up ⅛ of an inch for every inch the waist increases in size; so that for a figure 36 chest, and 35 waist, there would only be ½ an inch taken out at this part. If the waist becomes very large, then disproportion should be used in the manner explained fully in Part II, "Cutter's Practical Guide".

From 9¼ to 21 is 3 inches over the half chest measure, which will not be found any too much; indeed, another half inch may be added without detriment, for it must be borne in mind how thick this velveteen is, and also the thickness of the lining, which should be either Tweed or Woollen Plaid. The front shoulder is also ½ an inch larger and the over shoulder 1 inch larger than for the ordinary coat, but this is as much for the extra shoulder development of the wearer as anything, so that if the measures are taken direct on the customer it will not be necessary to add to them, though a little extra length of front shoulder would be advantageous.

The Skirt.

It will be noticed the construction line is dropped 1½ inches in front, with the result that more space appears between skirt and bodypart at waist, the top of skirt only coming ¾ of an inch above line at underarm seam. The back of the skirt is cut in the usual way. Large hare pockets are put on the inside of skirt, the full width of skirt, and arranged with two holes and buttons. There are two good-sized hip pockets, one on each skirt, with flaps of at least 10 inches wide and 3½ deep. There is an outside breast pocket, and one, if not two, inside ditto, so that it will be seen the pockets of this garment are a very important feature; and as they are all intended for heavy usage, they should be well stayed and made from stout material — Jean is the material mostly used for this purpose. The buttons generally used are sporting bronze. The front is sometimes made to fasten up to the throat and the neck finished with a Prussian collar. The cuff is finished with two holes and buttons. The shoulders are often strapped with either the same material or leather; when the latter is used it is put on after the garment is finished. If it is put on one shoulder only, then it would be put on the left and the size and position arranged to take the wear of the gun resting on that part.

MORNING COAT.
Plate 14. Diagram 30.

Livery servants are usually supplied with undress garments to wear at their work, &c. At stated intervals, Coachmen and Grooms have their Stable Suits and Footmen their Pantry Jackets, &c. We will now proceed to describe the special features of these.

The Trousers and Vests we have previously dealt with, so we have only to describe the Morning Coat as worn by Coachmen. It is usually cut rather forward in the skirt and made to button 3, has flaps and pockets on the hips and inside breast pockets. An outside breast pocket would not be in harmony with the general rules followed for Livery garments.

The material used for this is of the plainest description — a dark grey Derby Tweed, a plain Twill with ay a white spot, or a bird's-eye Check, or something of the neatest description. It must have good wearing qualities, as it is subjected to a pretty fair test in this respect.

The Cutting.

This is done on precisely the same lines as any other Morning Coat, and as this is a somewhat important garment and may be required for others as well as Coachmen, we will briefly lay down the system again.

We will assume the taking of the measures has been mastered, or if not then the proportion they bear to the chest acquired, so we will at once proceed to draw lines O 2½, O 32 at right angles; O to 3½ is one-third depth of scye plus ½ inch; O to 9 the depth of scye; O to 17 the natural waist; O to 19 the fashion waist; O to 32 the full length desired, plus two seams. Draw lines at right angles to these points as illustrated; O to 2½ is one-twelfth breast, minus ½ inch; about 2 inches below 3½ apply the width of back, plus ½ inch for seams. At 17 come in 1 inch and draw back seam; from ½ to 20½ the half chest measure, plus 2 to 2½ inches according to the thickness of the material or the ease desired in the garment; from 20½ to 12½ measure back the across chest measure and proceed to sweep for the neck point F, using the front shoulder minus the back neck for the first sweep from 12½, and adding an inch to it when sweeping from 20½ as indicated by 13½. To find point D the over shoulder measure is used, deducting the distance ½ W of the back from it, and by the remainder sweeping from 12½, putting the finger on the tape 1½ inches up before sweeping as illustrated by dotted line 17. From these points the shoulder and scye may be drawn, using the diagram as a guide for the shape, &c. It will be noticed the back is a little short of the sidebody; this should be so to the extent of a ¼ inch. The correct length may be got by sweeping from point ¾ on line 9 from a point ¼ inch above the back sideseam.

The Position of the Seams

Is found as follows: The width of back scye and back at waist are both one-ninth of the half breast; a line is drawn from 17 to the top of sideseam, and the back is hollowed ¾ of an inch, and completed as shown. Now use the top of sideseam as a pivot, and sweep from A to find the proper length of sidebody at bottom. Take out 1½ inches between 3 and 4½, varying it — more for prominent blades and less for flat blades. Continue below 4½ at right angles to line 17, 21; from the bottom of sidebody at hip button draw a line across at right angles to line O 19, which is used for a guide to get the waist seam. The underarm seam is got by measuring from point ½ one-fourth breast, squaring down and taking out ½ inch on either side of this line. Now measure up the size of waist from 1 to 3, 4½ to 9, and 10 to 21, making it the same amount over the waist as ½ 20½ is over the chest. The breast line may now be drawn, starting from V (which is one-twelfth breast minus ½ inch from point F) through 20½, to 21. Now shape the gorge by making V a pivot and sweeping from F, and then shaping the lapel in accordance with taste. Add on a button-stand of 1¼ inches, and run the front to taste. Hollow the waist seam 1 inch above line drawn from hip button, and if the waist seam is desired fairly low in front the forepart may be dropped ½ or 1 inch below this line.

The Skirt.

This is produced by squaring down from lower waist line at right angles as to 9, and coming out 1 inch as shown, drawing a line from hip button through 1 to bottom, adding on ½ inch of round and allowing 1 inch extra length for making up. Come above the line at waist ¾ of an inch, and draft the top as shown, taking in a little bit at front, and drafting the rest in harmony with the front. The flap on the hip is made about 9 inches wide and placed a trifle nearer the back than the front; the top edge of the flap is cut straight, which does away with any necessity for fulling it on in the same way as the skirt is done. If a fuller style of skirt is required so as to provide more room for the pockets, drop the line by which you square down at right angles to 9, say ¾ or 1 inch in the way illustrated on Diagram 29, which will produce a greater opening between the top of skirt and the bottom of the body part. The edges of these coats are generally single stitched.

LOUNGE FOR COACHMAN & GROOM.
Plate 15.

For stable wear, the Groom generally has a Lounge in preference to the Morning Coat in our last; and as this is a garment largely used in nearly every sphere of life, we have no doubt our readers will find this Diagram and the following explanation of general use.

In connection with Stable Clothes, it will be well for the tailor to make a note in his diary as to when the various servants' Liveries falls due and remind them. They appreciate the attention, and it frequently brings in an order for a suit at a time when trade is slack, and you are glad of it to keep your men going.

All that we have said with reference to the material and the plainness of the pattern and trimmings applies equally to the Lounge as the Morning Coat, and similar features should be introduced as regards the style.

It should not be cut away too smartly, or on the other hand must it be made clumsy. The Diagram gives a very good medium style in this respect. Then, as regards pockets, the ordinary hip and ticket pockets are put in with flaps, but the breast pocket is better put inside. By this we do not mean that it is positively forbidden to be put outside, but that it introduces a smartness that is inconsistent with Livery details generally.

The Cutting. Diagram 31.

We will now proceed to place the system briefly before our readers, and in doing so we would remark that the system will work just as well for an ordinary Lounge as for one intended only for Livery wear, the variations being more matters of style than fit.

Draw lines O 2½, O 29; from O to 3½ is one-third depth of scye plus ½ inch; O to 9 is depth of scye; O to 17 is natural waist; O to 29 is full length plus seams; draw lines at right angles to these points; hollow for back seam ⅜ of an inch at natural waist, and mark off on the various lines as follows: O to 2½ one-sixth of the neck, or, failing that measure, one-twelfth of breast minus ½ inch; come up ¾ of an inch from this point and shape back neck about 2 inches below point 3½; mark off the width of the back as taken on the customer, plus two seams (½ inch), and shape back scye and shoulder seams of back as illustrated, slightly hollowing the shoulder seam between W and ¾. From the backseam on line 9 measure forward to 20¾ the half chest measure plus 2½ inches; from 20¾ measure back to 12¾ the across chest measure; and having by this means found the front of scye, proceed to apply the front shoulder measure taken as described in the Appendix. The mode of using it is as follows: Deduct O ¾ of the back neck from the front shoulder measure, and by the remainder sweep, using 12¾ as a pivot, and sweeping to get point F

as illustrated by the dotted lines 12½ Now add 1 inch to this quantity and sweep again, but this time using point 20¾ as the pivot, the sweeps crossing each other gives the proper position of the neck point F. The next measure to apply is the over shoulder measure, which is done as follow: First measure from the back seam at 9 to W as per dotted line; deduct this quantity from the over shoulder and by the remainder sweep, putting the one end of the tape at 12¾, but making a pivot 1½ inches above, which is done by laying the tape down and putting the finger on it 1½ inches above 12¾; the measure is by this means applied as taken. The width of the shoulder F D is made ¼ inch less than the back, and now the scye may be drafted. The scye should touch the line squared up from 12¾ 1½ inches up, it should touch line 9 20¾ 1½ inches back from 12¾, and the hollow should not be more than ¾ of an inch from point 12¾. The back scye should be kept as close up as possible and the forepart arranged, so that when the sideseam is sewn, it will not be necessary for the man to drop down the back before he can get a seam. The placing of the sideseam comes next, and in this there is scope for a considerable amount of taste. In our own practice we usually make the back one-sixth of the breast as from ⅜ to 6⅜, and square down from this point at right angles to line 17 to bottom of sideseam, running it upwards from this point into the scye in the style shown in Diagram.

Suppress the waist 1 inch from 6⅜ to 7⅜, and draft sideseam of forepart as illustrated, letting the forepart overlap the back ½ an inch as shown. Now take out the fish under the arm if it is desired to fit closely; take out 1 inch, placing the back of the fish 3 inches from the sideseam at both chest and waist and letting it terminate about 4 inches below the waist line. Now measure up the size of the waist, allowing the same amount over the waist measure as was allowed over the chest. The breast line or the meeting-edge-to-edge line will be the next to draw, and this is got by coming out from F to V the same as O 2½ of the back, and drawing a line from V through 20¾ and 21. The gorge is drawn by coming down from V to I 2½ to 3 inches, or about the same as V F. It only remains to add on a button-stand of 1¼ inches, and to draft the outline of the front, but in doing this it will be well to measure from 9 to 29 of the back, and make the bottom of front (A) ¾ of an inch more from line 20¾ than the measure taken on the back.

The position of the pockets and the style of the lapel are clearly brought on in the Diagram, so that if our readers follow these details they will not go far wrong. he sleeve is described on the next page.

FOOTMAN'S PANTRY JACKET.
Plate 16. Diagram 32.

A glance at the Diagram will show this is cut on the lines of a Lounge, with the back on the crease and the front arranged with a low turning roll of the D.B. type. They are usually made from striped Jean, and lined with cotton, so that they may be easily washed, which operation they have to frequently undergo. Pockets are put in, one on either forepart, and finished with a welt about 6 inches long and ⅞ to 1 inch wide. Like all garments intended to be frequently washed, it is made up with the least possible interlining, and the buttons are made up on brass rings from the same material; there are generally three buttons, and they turn to about a couple of inches above the waist in the style illustrated. There are several variations of this garment, but this is looked upon as the standard style. One variation is to make a roll collar instead of the pointed turn, but this is not often used. For Page boys, however, this garment is made to fasten up to the throat with a stand collar and minus pocket, it being considered inad-

visable to increase the receptacles for an accumulation of rubbish, &c., in boys' garments.

As will be gathered from the Diagram, the stripes of the material are arranged to run vertically or up and down the figure.

The Cutting. Diagram 32.

For the general working of the system, we refer our readers to the Lounge on previous page, where it is fully explained; so if we just note the variations practiced for these garments that will be sufficient. In the first place, as the back is cut on the crease, nothing can be taken out from the back construction line. In marking off the width of back, add only one seam instead of two. The width of back at the waist is made one-eighth breast instead of one-sixth, and 1½ inches is taken out between back and fore-part instead of 1 inch. This is illustrated on line 17 from 4½ to 6. As it is not intended for this garment to fit into the waist closely, the fish is not taken out under the arm, but that amount is allowed extra over the waist measure, so that in measuring up the waist, fully 3 inches is allowed over the half waist measure. It will be noticed 2½ inches is allowed over the chest measure, the reason being that it is a working garment and being frequently in the wash-tub it may possibly shrink a trifle. The usual length of these garments is about 6 inches below the waist, and they are cut to come straight round at the bottom, an inlay being generally put at that part so as to prevent the lining coming below the bottom in the course of wear. We now turn our attention to

The System for Sleeves. Diagram 33.

It being of the first importance that the sleeve should be cut in harmony with the scye into which it is to go, we take all the measures from that part of the jacket. First square a line up from the depth of scye line

9 to the most backward point of the scye, as illustrated at 7¼ of Diagram 32, and from this point measure across to the front of scye at 12½; this quantity finds the distance from the top of the sleeve head to the top of forearm seam; the mode of applying it to the draft is shown by Diagram 33 from O to 5¼ The next thing is to get the balance of the sleeve, which is done by first marking the pitches: the forearm pitch should be placed ¾ of an inch above the level of scye as illustrated at V. The hindarm pitch is fixed to taste, a very good guide being 2 inches below the shoulder seam or one-eighteenth breast. Having arranged the pitches, take your square and place its opposite arms, one at each pitch as illustrated on Diagram, arranging the arm over the forepart in the position it is desired the sleeve shall hang when in the garment. In all Livery garments the sleeve should hang well forward, as Coachmen's arms are always forward in the act of driving, and Footmen have to continually bring their arms forward whilst waiting at the table. Having arranged the square in the desired position, notice what is opposite the forearm pitch, and apply that quantity from 5¼ to 1 of the sleeve, and draw line across to find the top of the hindarm. Now place the back and forepart together in a closing position at the shoulder seam, and measure the distance from back pitch to front pitch in a straight line, and whatever that is, apply from 1 to 8¾. O to 4¼ is half-way across. Draw a line from 4¼ to 5¼, and round the sleeve head ¾ of an inch as shown, completing the sleeve head by a continuous curve to 8¾. Now mark off the length of the sleeve, allowing as a general rule for three seams ¾ of an inch, though in the case of a whole back for two seams ½ an inch. Now mark off the elbow and cuff; hollow the forearm 1 inch at elbow as shown; and for Undercoats make the width of elbow about 1 inch less than one-fourth of the breast, and for Overcoats, &c., fully ½ inch more,

that being a very good guide, the measure being applied from 1 to 9. The width of the cuff is made in like manner one-sixth breast for Undercoats and ½ to ¾ of an inch wider for Overcoats. The run of the bottom of the cuff may be got by using the top the hindarm as a pivot and sweeping forward from 6, or it may be got by squaring from 9 6. The shape of the hindarm is illustrated. A little round is added outside a straight line drawn from 6 to 9, and a little hollow is made between 8¾ and 9. For the underside sleeve, measure round the bottom part of the scye between the two pitches, and apply that measure from 5¼ as shown by 7½. Hollow the underpart as shown, getting the top of underarm by using 9 as a pivot and sweeping from 8¾. Complete the hindarm as shown.

This sleeve system applies to all the garments in the book, inlays being left at the cuff for buttons as required.

LIVERY OVERCOATS.
Plate 17. Diagram 34.

The old Box Coat has now become a thing of the past, and in its place we have the Livery Overcoat, a garment of the D.B. Frock Coat style, buttoning up to the neck and finished with Prussian collar. The skirts are made long and full. The material mostly used for this is Devon, the favourite colour being drab although it is by no means confined to that shade, the regulation in this respect being of the same colour as the carriage lining, hence a large number are made in browns and blues. The regulations as regards details are as follows: —

The length of the Coachman's Coat is made to come to the middle part of the top boots. There are flap pockets on the hips, the size of the flaps being about 10½ by 3¾. A ticket pocket is put either in the waist-seam, or in the forepart as shown, a flap being put to go in or out.

The length of the Footman's Overcoat is to be within 6 or 7 inches of the ground. The pockets are placed in the pleat, so that there are no flaps on the hips, and if a ticket pocket is inserted it is put in the waistseam. The Groom's Overcoat is very much like the Coachman's, with the exception that it comes just below the knee only, the pockets being put on the hips with flaps, &c.

On all Overcoats a side edge is put, 12 inches long, in the manner shown on the Diagram, with three buttons, one at bottom, one in the middle, and one on the top of the pleat. This side edge is merely a piece of material placed on the back skirt and stitched on and then sewn in with the pleat

They are all made with six buttons up each front, the top one being arranged so that it will just go over the bottom of the collar and keep its end in place. The bottom button is generally placed in the waistseam, but not always; the buttons not used for buttoning are plugged, that is, a hole is made with the bodkin at the part it is desired for the button to go and the shank of the button forced through it, and then a piece of canvas drawn through the eye of the shank. The edges are usually double stitched raw, the only variation being to single stitch them; the seams are generally left plain, but this is by no means universal, they being often slated and double-stitched.

As regards linings, the body part is usually lined with Tweed, the skirt lined with Shaloon, and the sleeve with plain Linen. The pockets are arranged as previously stated for the different servants, together with an inside breast pocket in the left breast.

The System of Cutting.

There are several variations from the ordinary system as previously explained, and these we will briefly state. On the back line points 3½ and 9 are as usual, but the natural and fashion waists are both increased ½ an inch. The back seam is drawn ½ an inch in from point 17½, and the width of back at waist is made one-twelfth breast, and only 1 inch taken out between back and sidebody. The width of back is increased 1 inch beyond the measure taken, the across chest measure is increased ⅜ of an inch, and 3½ inches is allowed beyond the actual chest and waist measures taken over the vest. The front shoulder is increased ½ an inch, and only ¾ of an inch is added to the front shoulder measure when making the second sweep. The reason for this reduction is the difficulty of working up this material. O to 3 of the back and F to V of the forepart are both made the full one-twelfth of the breast, and the bottom of the gorge may be found the same distance down from V, or it may be made a trifle lower, as these servants often desire to wear a muffler round their neck under this coat, and consequently the neck requires to be enlarged to allow this.

The lapel is cut with the sewing-to-edge the same as the front of the forepart is made, about 2½ inches wide at the top and bottom, the outer edge being drawn straight; the top of the lapel is drawn down, so that the top hole may come near the top, and as the buttons are arranged as previously stated for the end of the collar to go under the top button, this is the only way it can be arranged.

The skirt is arranged with a considerable increase in the drapery at the sides, and this is done by coming down from 3 to 3½ inches at A, using the former quantity for Footmen and the latter amount for Coach-men, who require a fuller skirt from their position on the box. Draw a line from A to the hip button, and square down at right angles to it 9 inches and come out 1, and draw a line through to bottom, beyond which add ½ an inch of round. Mark off the length by allowing 1 inch for making up. From line drawn from A to hip button come up ¾ of an inch at ¾, and continue waist-seam across as illustrated.

To get the run of front, come up from top of skirt to * the same distance as A is below it, and having marked off the width of skirt by the size of sidebody, forepart and lapel, plus ¾ inch, square the front edge at right angles to * and the hip button. Make the length of the front of the skirt the same as the back, and complete as per diagram.

The sleeve should be cut ½ an inch wider at elbow and cuff and ½ an inch longer than ordinary measure; care should also be taken to avoid getting too much fullness in the sleeve head. The cuff is generally finished with five rows of stitching.

The collar is cut as per diagram at bottom of the skirt; draw line O 8 and make it the size of neck; from 8 come up to 1, 1 inch, and draw sewing to edge of collar; O to 1¼ depth of stand desired, and draw crease row as illustrated, marking the outline below this to taste, usually about 2 inches or 2¼ deep. In making this collar, the stand and fall are often cut separate, the stand being cut as an ordinary stand collar, and fall as the lower part of the diagram, though it frequently happens the fall is not lined except just at the edge, wide enough to take the stitching, and this undoubtedly has an advantage in thinness. It will be found necessary to lower the left gorge one seam, or it will not appear level in front when finished. On another page we illustrate how to take it out of the cloth, so we need not dwell on it here, and the only point requiring further mention is the need there is for special care to keep it clean in the process of making, and this cannot be emphasized too strongly.

UNOFFICIAL COURT DRESS.
Plate 18. Diagrams 35 and 36.

Inasmuch as every true and loyal citizen is a servant of the State, we may look upon Court Dress as the livery of the Court, being worn in one of the two styles — official or unofficial — described in this work, by all gentlemen attending Her Majesty's Drawing Rooms, State Concerts, Court Balls, and such like occasions.

Unofficial Court Dress is worn on these occasions by all those who have no official position under the State, such as the Army, the Navy, or Civil Service; and as this class is much more varied than the other, consequently the ordinary cutter is far more likely to get an order for them.

There are two kinds of Unofficial Court Dress, though the cut of both are alike, the outline of which may be gathered from the Diagram; the run of front is one of the most important parts, and if our readers follow the Diagram in this particular they will not go far wrong. The body part is cut as an ordinary Dress Coat, and the fronts also are very similar; the gorge is lowered from the Frock Coat model, and the top and bottom of breast cut off, whilst just in the centre a little round is added. Buttons are put on up the right forepart and sham notched holes made of edging cord put up the left, the length of the hole being 1¼ inches. The skirt, as will be seen, is of the Dress Coat type, the usual rules as regards length and width of strap and bottom being applied here, whilst the total length is also similar to the Dress Coat. We need not further dwell on the cutting of Court Dress, as with these few hints and what can be gathered from the Diagram — which like all the others in this work is drawn to the ¼ inch scale — we think our readers will find all they need in this respect, so we will proceed to describe the

Different kinds

Of Unofficial Court Dress. As we have already pointed out, they are cut as a S.B. Dress Coat with a stand collar, the fronts cut just large enough to meet at the roundest part, but as they are never worn buttoned it is not cut large enough to allow for this. There are eight gilt buttons used, six up the front and two on the hips, though this number should be increased by some on the cuffs and under each point of the flap; but inasmuch as these are not generally used now, we have illustrated the prevailing style.

The collar, cuffs, and flaps are trimmed with gold embroidery, and for the benefit of those of our readers who know nothing about these garments, we may say the correct thing in embroidery, buttons, swords, and all kinds of fittings and trimmings can be obtained of such firms as Messrs. Firmin & Sons or Jones & Co., of Golden Square, who make a speciality of supplying the regulation patterns of these goods.

The cloth used for the Coat is a dark mulberry Superfine; the material used for the Waistcoat is white Marcella, the style being single-breasted, no collar, opening low, and only four gilt buttons; whilst the Trousers are made from the same cloth as the Coat, with a row of gold lace placed down the sideseams.

Breeches take the place of Trousers on certain occasions, such as Drawing Rooms, concerts, and balls. They are made from the same cloth, and finished with three buttons at the knee.

As regards the Cocked Hat, the Cockade, the Sword, the Belt, &c , we need not enter into detailed description, as these the tailor would procure from firms such as those mentioned above.

Another kind of this dress is made from black Silk Velvet, with cut steel buttons and fittings. The Velvet is used for the Coat and Breeches, but the Vest is made of white Marcella as above. Black Patent Leather Shoes and black Silk Stockings cover the lower part of the leg, the buckle on the shoes as well as all the other fittings being made of steel in the place of gilt.

Trousers are sometimes made of black Silk Velvet for Levees and dinners, but they are the exception.

A small white necktie is worn with both kinds of Dress. The lining used for the Velvet Coat is white, Silk, Serge, or Satin being the materials mostly used; for the Cloth Coat it is generally black. We have endeavoured to make the Diagram as explicit in matters of detail as possible, whilst in the matter of fitting the customer the usual rules as prev-iously explained must be applied, so we will proceed to give the following extract from the *Tailor and Cutter* on

The Cost of Court Dress.

"An editor if he goes to a Court Ball as a plain civilian can get his clothes for a mere song as compared with some of the official dresses. If he writes a cheque for £24, he will get in exchange a Silk Velvet Dress Coat, Vest and Breeches to match — Oh! if he has only fine calves. A Cocked Hat with steel loop and a sword. How much at home he will look with a sword between his legs! If he desires to plaster himself all over with steel buttons they will be an extra, but as he can get them large size for 13/- a dozen and small size for 11/6, what a quantity he will be able to get for a £5 note".

On the next page we give other extracts showing the cost of Official Court Dress, which items will doubtless be of interest, if not of service, to our readers, who must always remember these are the retail prices.

OFFICIAL COURT DRESS.
Plate 19. Diagrams 37, 38, and 39.

We now treat of the Official Court Costumes as worn by members of the Ministerial, Diplomatic, and Civil Services on such State occasions as Drawing Rooms, Balls, and Concerts of State. The members of these services are divided into five classes,

but only the first and second have *full* Dress Coats, with the exception of those engaged in the Queen's household, in which case it is extended to the third class. The variation for the different classes is more a question of trimming and embroidery than anything else; the shape of the Coat, and this is what mostly concerns the cutter, is the same in all cases. This, as will be seen from Diagram 37, is a single-breasted Coat, and for the first and second classes this is made to fasten up the front with hooks and eyes and finished at the neck with a stand collar. This style may also be worn by the third class of the Queen's household; for the Semi-state first and second class, and is the only one used by the lower classes. It is made to button up the front with nine buttons, in which case due allowance must be made for the button-stand, say ⅝ on the hole side and 1¼ on the button side. The width of the embroidery varies in the following manner for the different classes. For the first-class it is made 5 inches wide; the second 4 inches wide and has a saw edge, which applies also to the lower classes; the third 3 inches wide; the fourth 2 inches wide; and the fifth an edging ⅜ of an inch wide. The Semi-state Coat is embroidered on flaps, cuffs, collar, and back, with two buttons on hips and two in the pleats, and is lined with back Silk. Variations are also made in the other details of the costume, such as the sword, hat, &c., so as to be in harmony.

The Cutting.

In cutting these garments there are one or two points to be observed: First, the back is cut on the crease and stumped, or in other words the back skirts sewn on at the bottom. The hindarm of the sleeve is arranged to come to the sidebody seam, and consequently the shoulder seam is kept fairly high, so that generally it partakes very much of the military style of cut. The material from which these garments are made is blue cloth, and it goes almost without saying that great care is necessary in making them, those engaged in the regular military trade being the most successful. The garment is got ready for trying on in the usual way, and when the fit has been arranged satisfactorily, it is sent to one of the firms who make a speciality of embroidering these garments, and who generally have a staff of specialists for this branch of the trade, and they do all that is necessary in the embroidery way; so that, elaborate as these garments undoubtedly are, it is not such a difficult matter for the tailor as at first sight would be imagined, really amounting to very little more than making an ordinary coat. The Breeches worn with this costume are made from white Kerseymere, with covered buttons at the knees and buckles of gilt material. The stockings are of white Silk, and the patent leather shoes have gilt buckles. We need not enter into details of sword, belt, cocked hat, &c., as these will always be obtained from such firms as we have previously mentioned, and who make a point of always supplying their customers with the correct thing. The lining used for the Full Dress first class Coat, including flaps and cuffs, should be of white Silk, though sometimes black is used for this purpose, the latter colour being used for the Semi-state Coat. Both the State and Semi-state Coats are finished with black Silk Velvet collars and cuffs, except in the Queen's household when they are made of scarlet cloth.

The pattern of the embroidery may be gathered from the Diagram, which is of a first-class Full Dress Coat. There are nine gilt-mounted buttons put up the fronts and two at the back on the hips. Trousers made from blue cloth, with lace 2½ inches wide placed down the side, are worn with the Semi-state Coat.

A Coat such as we have dealt with of the first class would probably cost £80, the full outfit; amounting up to about £100. These items are taken from the same source as the extract dealing with Unofficial Court Dress on the previous page.

We have not dealt with Court Dress for Military and Naval Officers, as that is only the full dress uniform of their respective ranks, full particulars of which will be found in "The Dress Regulations of Her Majesty's Army" and the companion book found in the "Quarterly Navy List".

The officials entitled to wear first class Uniform are the President of the Board of Control, Chancellor of the Exchequer, First Lord of the Treasury, First Lord of the Admiralty, Secretary at War (being in the Cabinet), President of the Council, Lords of the Privy Council, Lord Privy Seal, President of the Board of Trade, Secretaries of State, Chief Commissioner of Woods and Forests (if in the Cabinet), Ambasadors (with an embroidered sleeve and backseam), Chancellor of the Duchy of Lancaster, Postmaster General (being in the Cabinet), and the Lord Chancellor.

The officers of the Household entitled to wear the first class uniform are: The Lord Chamberlain of the Household, The Lord Great Chamberlain, The Lord Steward, Gentlemen of the Stole, and the Comptroller.

The Captain of the Gentlemen-at-Arms, The Captain of the Yoemen of the Guard, The Master of the Horse, The Master of the Buck Hounds, The Squires and the Pages of Honour have special uniforms appointed for them.

COACHMAN'S STATE LIVERY.
Plate 20. Diagram 40.

On this and the succeeding plate we deal with State and Semi-State Livery, as worn by servants in large families; and in doing so we do not think we can do better than describe this kind of livery that was made for a recent Lord Mayor of London.

Velvet and Gold are rather expensive materials to deal with, and so it is necessary to take every care in getting the order correctly, and on the occasion above quoted a water colour illustration was prepared showing, the detail of the embroidery and trimming distinctly, and submitted to the Lord Mayor for his approval. This being done, an accurate guide is obtained to work to.

The Coats on this occasion were made of Royal Blue Velvet embroidered with dead gold, the pattern of which has been transferred to our diagram sheet; and, as will be seen, it consists of fleur-de-lis intertwined with ivy. The edges of the Coat and flaps and the sideseam were trimmed with gold lace, the diamonds showing darker on the diagram were of red cloth. The lace used varies in price from 5/- to 15/2 per yard, and takes a long time to make, and on occasions of this sort when time is limited, it presents a difficulty, as owing to its liability to tarnish it is never kept in stock and quantities, and in making it the lacemen have to set up their looms specially for each pattern, and the operative is only able to furnish from 2½ to 3 yards per day.

The Cutting

of these garments is very similar to a Morning Coat. The gorge is slightly lowered, and the front is rounded so as to get the roundest part to come to the most prominent part of the figure, and fasten with two hooks and eyes arranged alternately, that is one hook and one eye on either forepart. The amount to allow for making up must certainly not be less than 2 inches, 2½ would probably be better, as it is not wise to make these garments too close fitting. The run of the front varies for Coachmen and Footmen in accordance with the varied position occupied on the state carriage, the Coachman sitting and Footman mounted behind and standing. Hence, in order to produce harmony in the outline of the two, the Coachman's is cut very much squarer or more forward than the Footman's. Dia. 40 illustrates the run of the front of the Coachman's, whilst Dia. 41 shows the Footman's. The difference between the state and semi-state being more a question of material than of outline.

The cuffs vary considerably. On the occasion quoted the cuffs were of the gauntlet form, but they are frequently slashed in similar style to the cuffs on naval uniforms, but this is a detail that must be in harmony with customers' wishes, in the same way as the pattern of embroidery. Amongst other details we notice

The Badge on the Sleeve,

which was quite an elaborate piece of embroidery, representing the Lord Mayor's coat-of-arms, and which was placed on the top side of the sleeve just above the elbow, and which, together with the embroidery on the gauntlet cuff and the bullion hanging from the epaulette, made the sleeve look half covered with gold. The epaulettes were of special pattern, and arranged to come just on the top of shoulder, which position is best found by putting the Coat on some one of as near the build of the wearer as possible, and arranging it accordingly. These epaulettes are now put on by means of metal fasteners — loops of metal as secured to the shoulders of the Coat, and a strap of metal is arranged under the epaulette, to be passed through and fastened up at the collar. This method is a distinct advance on the old style of working eyelet holes at neck and scye end of shoulder, which is now seldom used. As we may not refer again to epaulettes, we may as well here state that the semi-state garments were trimmed here with twisted cords.

The Vest and Breeches.

We give a diagram of the Full Dress Vests on the plate dealing with Footmen's Vests. In the present instance it was made from White

Cassimere, and laced and embroidered with gold to match the coat. The Breeches were made from White Buckskin, whole falls, and finished at knee with lace and buckles, above which were placed three buttons, and below it hung the tab.

The Coat was lined through with white, the body part being creased and dented for four diamonds. And here we may say it is customary to line the Coat the same colour as the Breeches and Vest are made.

The Hat and Wig would be obtained from their respective makers. The style of both may be gathered from the illustration.

A Rosette, termed a queue or cue, is worn on the back of the collar seam. This is supposed to represent the finishing tie of the tail of the Wig, but is in no way secured to that part.

FOOTMAN'S SEMI-STATE LIVERY.
Plate 21. Diagrams 41 and 42.

The variation between the outline of the Coachman's Full Dress Livery and the Footman's is here clearly illustrated, and, as will be seen, consists in the amount cut away above and below the part fastening with hooks and eyes just below point 20½; and as the Diagram is quite sufficient to illustrate this, we may proceed to describe the making, &c., in detail.

As the last Plate was a reproduction of. the State Livery used by a recent Lord Mayor, so this is a copy of his Semi-state Livery.

The Coat and Vest on this occasion were made of dark blue cloth, with the edges trimmed with gold Vandyke lace traced behind with Russia braid, which also formed five fern-leaf patterns across the breast, the top

one extending almost to the shoulder seam and the bottom one about 4 inches from the edge; Vandyke flaps, trimmed to correspond, were put across the waist, the pockets being arranged in the pleats behind. The Diagram illustrates the mode of trimming the side-seam, back, and cuff; and as this is correct in detail, our readers could not do better than follow this, should they have a similar order to execute.

The Vest was of the same style of cut as Diagram 16, but made from blue cloth, the edges being laced and traced in harmony with the Coat. The Breeches of this suit were made of yellow Plush.

There are many

Varieties of Full Dress,

From the plain style devoid of any ornamentation except a piping of different coloured cloth, we come to those with notched holes across the front similar to a Judge's or Queen's Counsel's Dress Coat. The notched-holes are formed with pieces of cord laid about two-thirds across the breast, that is, when there are sets of holes on both foreparts, but when they are put on one forepart only they should be slightly shortened. In this latter case there would not be any buttons on the left forepart, but would be put on the edge of the right forepart. When there are notched holes put on both foreparts, the buttons are placed at the end of holes.

An aigulette is sometimes worn on the left shoulder. This, as most of our readers are aware, is an ornament of cord, some of it plaited, fastened to the neck at back. As will be noticed on the Diagram, the cuff was finished with a gauntlet trimmed with lace, &c., in harmony with the fronts, &c., but this is by no means the universal way, they being often finished with slashed cuffs after the manner of a Naval Officer's Full Dress cuff, with the exception that the slash is generally placed about 2 inches from the

forearm seam and made about 4½ inches deep. A considerable variation may be made in the appearance of these garments by the mode of trimming — by this we mean the pattern of the braiding. On the Diagram it will be noticed the leaf pattern is made to run upwards at the same time as it runs across the breast, and this little variation would have the effect of making the figure look slightly taller by its modification of the effect of width produced by the lines running straight across the breast.

Some tailors put gold lace across the waist, but it must always be borne in mind that any decided line running round the figure in that way has the effect of making it appear shorter, and as Livery servants are seldom of the finest specimens of humanity, it will be well to avoid anything that makes them look shorter. The lining of Coats of this kind should be in harmony with the Breeches, &c., but on this feature the cutter had better use his judgment so that all may be produced in harmony.

It is hardly necessary for us again to repeat the particulars of Breeches, Silk Stockings, Buckle Shoes, &c., as all these are the same as for the Coachman, so that the only other feature we need notice is the Footman's

Footman's Cocked Hat.   Livery Dress Breeches.

Full Dress Hat, of which we give an illustration reduced from a photograph taken of one supplied to the Footman of a recent Lord Mayor. It was made from Silk Nap and trimmed with feathers and gold lace, and the view represented is the back. Footmen do not wear wigs but powder their hair, so the tailor will not have to take that article into consideration.

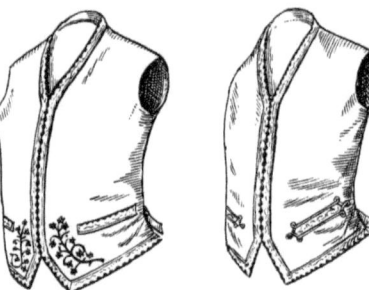

Livery State and Semi-State Vests.

COACHMAN'S MACINTOSH.
Plate 22. Diagram 44.

This being a standard work on the cutting and making all kinds of Livery garments, we have included this somewhat exceptional part of a Coachman's outfit in it. By exceptional, we mean it does not often fall to the ordinary tailor's lot to cut and make these, for inasmuch as they are loose-fitting garments, there is very little difficulty in getting ready-made garments to fit. And as the process of making up Macintosh goods is somewhat different to the ordinary method of making garments, the Tailor prefers to procure them from the Wholesale Manufacturer, many of whom advertise in the pages of the *Tailor and Cutter*. Their prices for these goods vary from 15/- to 25/-, so that the Tailor will be able to get a very good margin of profit on these goods, and leave the making up to those who make those goods a speciality. This garment is mostly cut with the sleeve seam running right up to the neck, though sometimes they are cut in the Sac style shown on the next page.

The Cutting.

Draw line O B O 12. From O to 2½ is ⅙ neck, or rather less than one-twelfth breast; O to 12 is ⅓ breast; 2½ to 27 the length of sleeve desired from the neck point; O to 10,

1 to 1½ inches more than ¼ breast; 10 to 11½, ¼ breast plus 2 to 2½ inches. From 2½ to 11½ is drawn by freehand, hollowing the forepart A slightly, say 1 inch more than the back at B. From 10 to 12 is 2 inches, and the side seam from 11½ to A is drawn at right angles to 12-11½. The length is marked off from 1 to B. The sleeve is draughted to follow the shoulder of front and back, with the exception that ½ inch is taken out between B and C, and the bottom part of sleeve made to overlap 11½, ¾. The width of sleeve is made to taste, and the under seam is drawn as shewn. The underarm seam is the only seam; the upper line, 2½ to 27, is cut on the crease. The gorge of the forepart is made by coming down from O to 3½, 1 inch more than O, 2½; and the forepart is finished by adding 2 inches beyond line O B, to act as overlap or button stand.

As will be gathered, this is a very easy-fitting garment, and is worn in lieu of the old style of Box Over Coat, to protect the wearer from the rain.

The Making of Macintoshes

is, as we have said, somewhat different to the ordinary method of garment making. They are cut so that there is as little fulness as possible, and then the seams are generally *stuck* together by a solution of rubber expressly prepared for the purpose, and which can be obtained from most of the Macintosh Manufacturers, or almost any Bicycle repairers. The edges are generally turned in and stuck together, and the pockets patched and stayed by sticking on round pieces, and the judicious use of string, in the same way that we use linen. Of recent years a large number of Macintoshes have been made up with stitched seams, a strapping being put over the seam on the inside to cover up the holes made by the needle in sewing. A piece of pure rubber or Macintosh, with a glaze surface, is put round the bottom of the Coat, and also round the bottom of the sleeves, to prevent the wet soaking upwards from the bottom, which it otherwise would do, on the same principle that a lamp wick soaks up the oil.

The Coachman's Macintosh is generally made from a white shining cloth, though occasionally they are made from black.

Three-Quarter Circle Cape.

Cloth Capes are very often worn by Coachmen, and Diagram 43 shows how they are cut. Take the back and forepart of these Overcoats and place them with the shoulder seams in a closing position, and mark round it, in that way coming out from the back 1 inch, as variation from dotted line at 17. Now mark off the length from W to 20, and make F to 6 the same length as the back plus ¾ inch; draw line A D level with the shoulder point, and make D 6 the same as A 20, and complete the run of the bottom by by freehand, from the points obtained.

These Capes are often arranged in tiers, as illustrated on Diagram 43, in which case they are seldom cut to extend right through, but the under one passes under the one above it about 3 or 4 inches, to which it is felled, though this plan is varied by cutting the bottom cape to extend right through to the neck, and the top one stitched to it. As will be gathered from the diagram, they are cut to run away in front, each cape showing a little more opening than the one below it. A tab is generally put at the bottom of the front of the bottom Cape to keep it from blowing up, and if the Capes are all cut to come through, they are fastened down at a little distance from the bottom corner by means of a little piece of Prussian binding, say about 3 inches long. The Cape is finished at the neck with a narrow band and 3 holes. They do not button down the front.

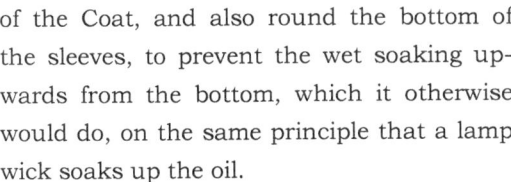

SAC OVER COAT.
Diagram 45. Plate 23.

The Sac Over Coat at one time figured prominently in Livery Garments, but now it is only occasionally, for such servants as the one illustrated on the plate, which is drawn from a Photograph of the Beadle of a recent Lord Mayor, the mace he is carrying in his hand being a historical curiosity; but as the details of the mace, &c., is foreign to our subject, we shall leave that for the Coat.

The Coat shewn on this figure was made from blue cloth and edged with gold lace, the fronts being cut to just meet edge and edge, so that the diagram would have to be reduced to line V I 21½ if used to produce a coat of this sort. It was cut to come to the knees, and had a Cape of the three-quarters-circle type, and long enough to reach to the elbow, which was also edged with gold lace. The folds forming in the Cape and Coat, and the looseness of the sleeves, gave it very much the appearance of a robe. It will be noticed the sleeve is trimmed up the forearm with gold lace made to form the outline of a slashed cuff.

The Old Style of Box Coat

Was cut on the same principle as is illustrated on this diagram only much fuller, the back being cut say 1½ to 2 inches beyond the construction line, and the forepart made to overlap the back from 3 to 4 inches, and so giving it any amount of width round the bottom of the skirt; it was cut long enough to reach to the ankle, and made to button all down the front, so,that the surplus width could be utilized to keep the legs of the Coachman warm in severe weather. On the top of this was worn a series of deep capes, such as we have described on page 50, Dia. Plate 22, they being often arranged so that every other one was of a different colour, such as brown and blue, &c., &c. They were generally finished at the neck with Prussian collar, the whole object of this garment being protection from the inclemency of the weather, and there can be no doubt it formed a very good one, although, as we have previously noted, Macintoshes and Driving Aprons have now taken its place; these are doubtless better for wet weather, but we think the Coachman exposed to the cold weather would prefer the old style.

The Cutting Diagram, 45.

This garment is cut on the principle of a Chesterfield, with the exception that the waist is made very easy fitting instead of defining the figure. The various points are found in the same way as described for the lounge, but as an Overcoat requires cutting longer in the front shoulder, it will be necessary to make the following additions to the various measures taken direct on the customer. The depth of scye is not altered. The natural waist is increased ⅜ inch. The front and over shoulder measures are increased ⅜ inch. The same amount being added to the across chest measure; and in drafting the scye let it come ½ an inch below the line as illustrated at ½. In measuring up the size of the chest allow 3½ to 4 inches over the half-chest measure, and square down at right angles; or if a full front is desired, draw a line from V through 21½ to bottom. From 17½ come out from back construction line ¾ inch, and draw centre of back straight so that it may be cut on the crease. From 17½ to 9 may be made ¼

breast, and the side seam of back drawn straight up and down at right angles to waist line, let the forepart overlap the back 1 to 1½ inches, as from 9 to 8, and draw sideseam of forepart straight through. In all other details follow the diagram. On the next page will be found a series of

Economy Lays

illustrating how the principal garments may be taken from the cloth advantageously, and we have no doubt these will be of special service to the cutter of limited experience in these garments. The Over Coat is arranged so that the skirts may be taken out without a whale piece, and this is done without in the slightest degree increasing the quantity of material. This is a plan that will be found very useful for Livery Over Coats and other Frock Coats of large size, where the skirts present a difficulty. And now we come to the

Conclusion.

And as we once more lay aside our pen for a rest, we do so with the hope that what we have now written in the present volume will prove a useful addition to our trade literature and help those desirous of mastering their profession to get a full and complete knowledge of the various garments worn for Livery, and as the source to find a concise explanation of systems for a large variety of garments used in every day wear.

THE AUTHOR.

Plates of Diagrams

ILLUSTRATING

THIS WORK.

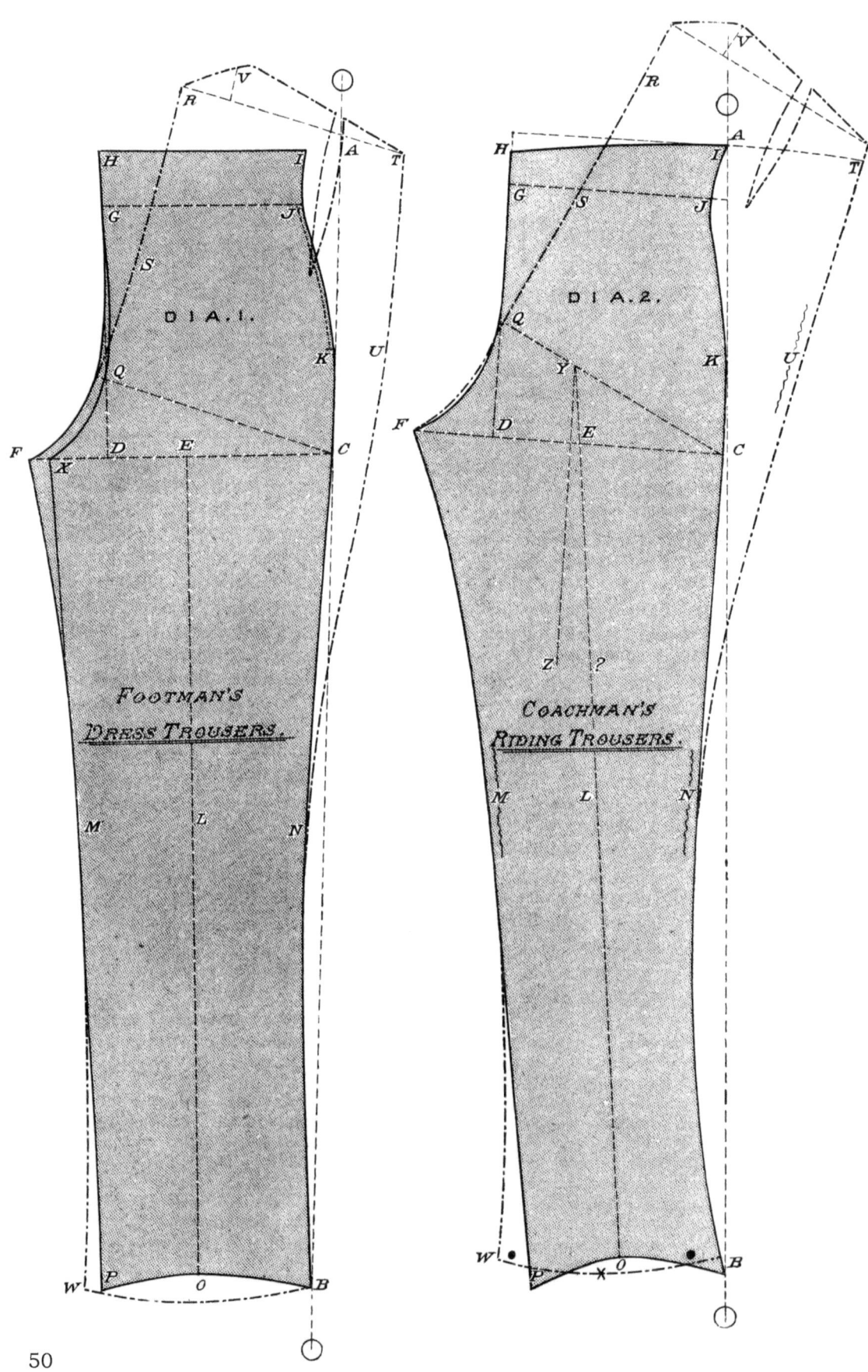

Plate 2.

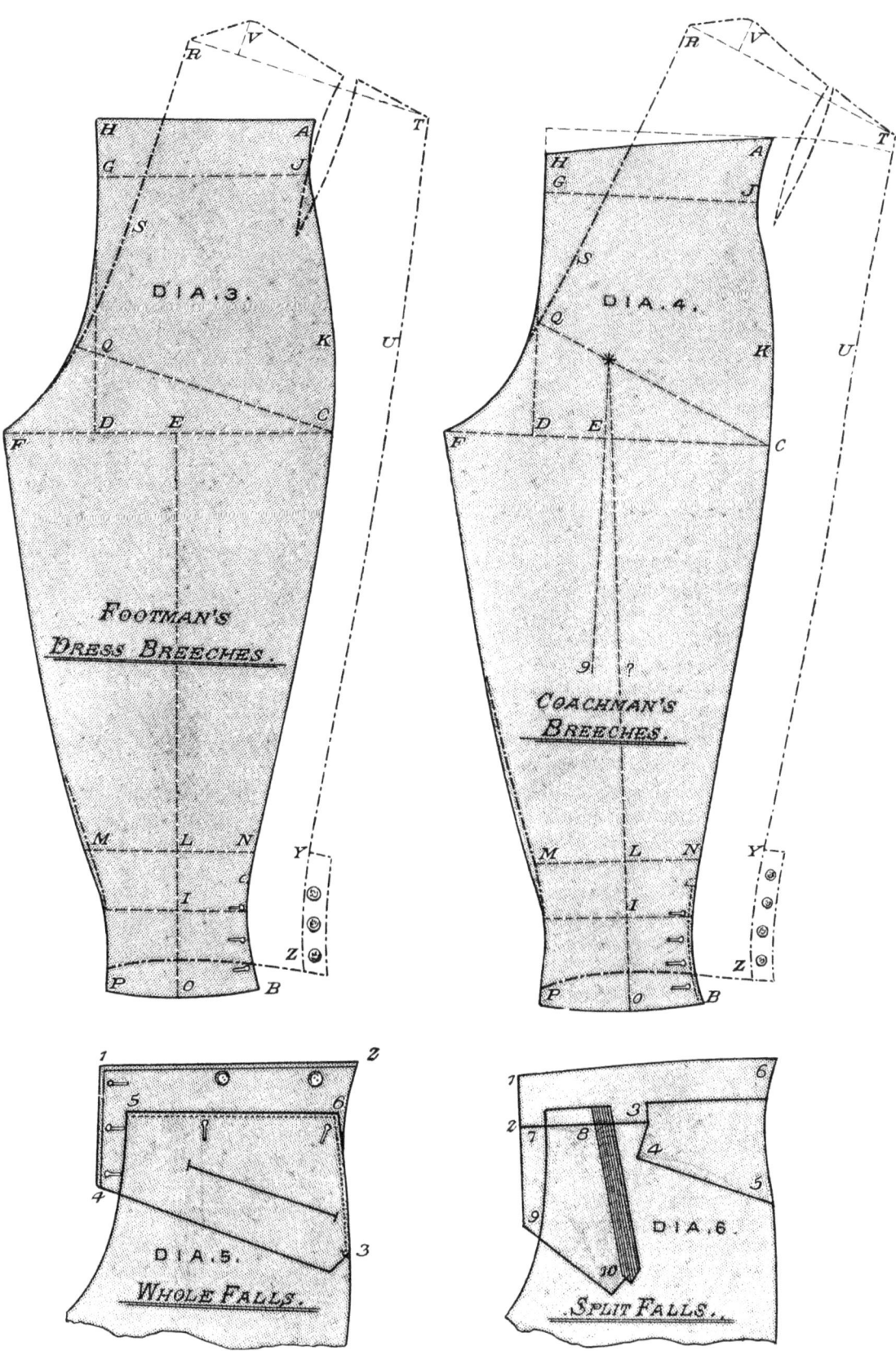

DIA.3.

FOOTMAN'S
DRESS BREECHES.

DIA.4.

COACHMAN'S
BREECHES.

DIA.5.

WHOLE FALLS.

DIA.6.

SPLIT FALLS.

Plate 3.

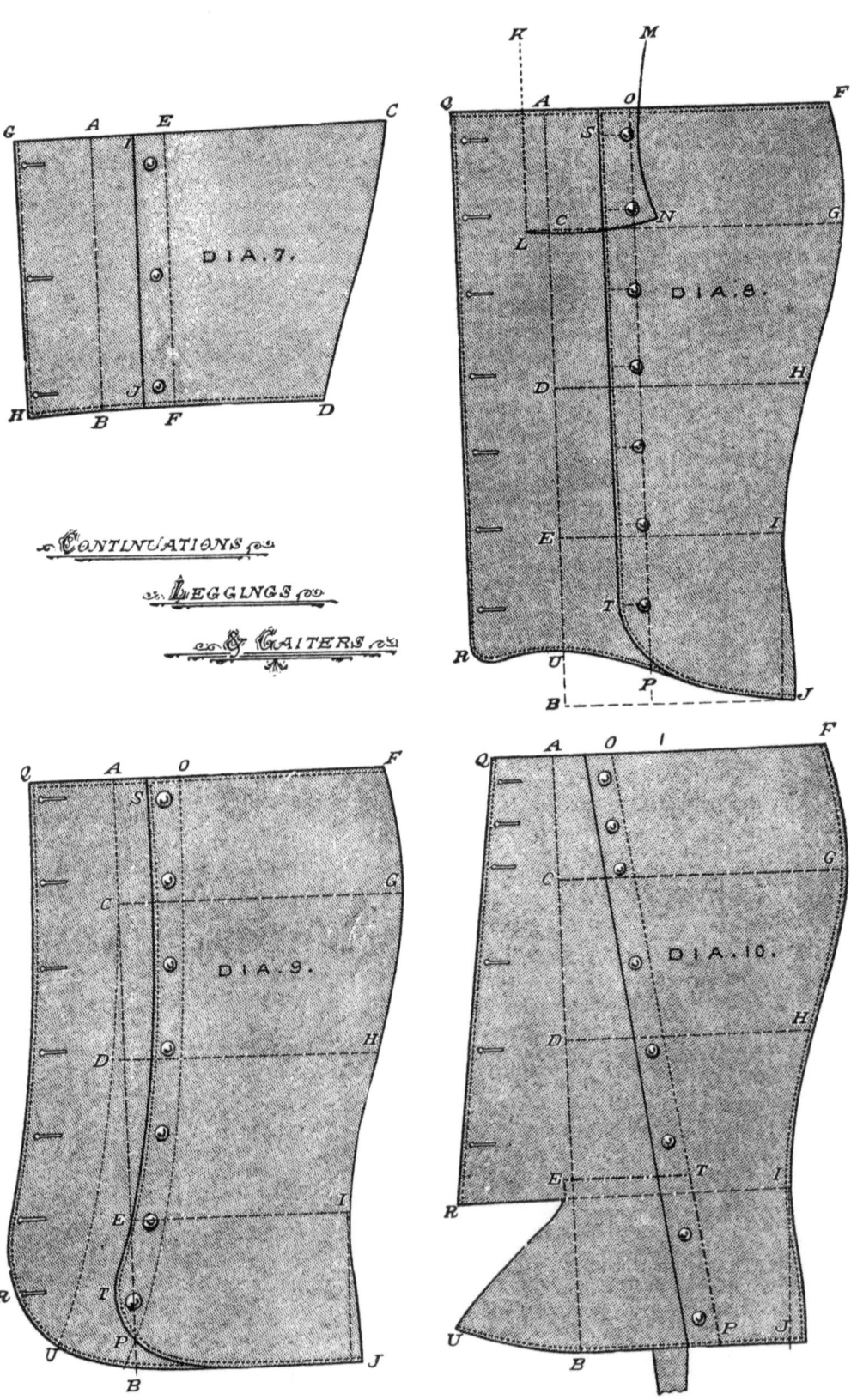

CONTINUATIONS

LEGGINGS

& GAITERS

DIA. 7.

DIA. 8.

DIA. 9.

DIA. 10.

Plate 4.

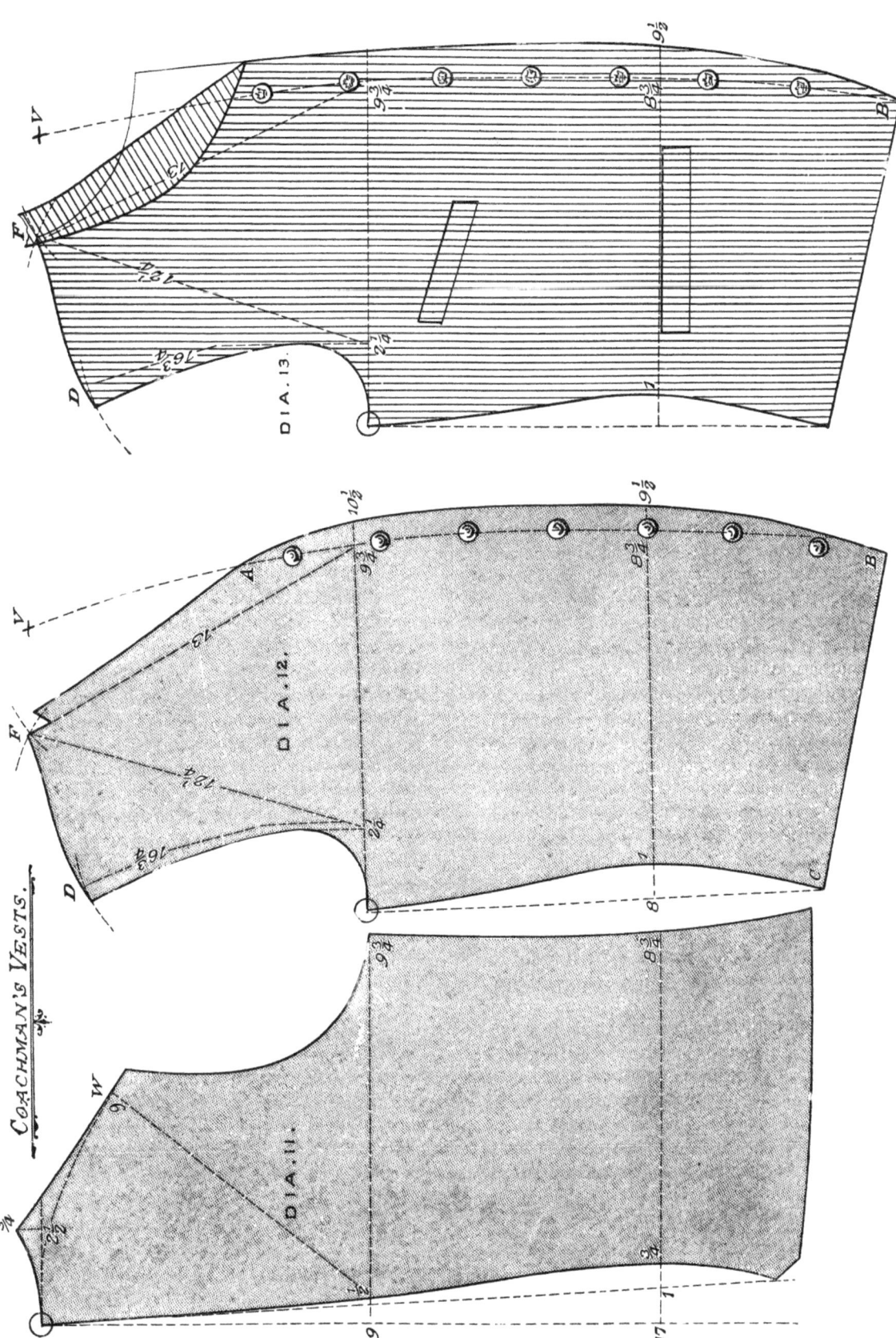

Plate 5.

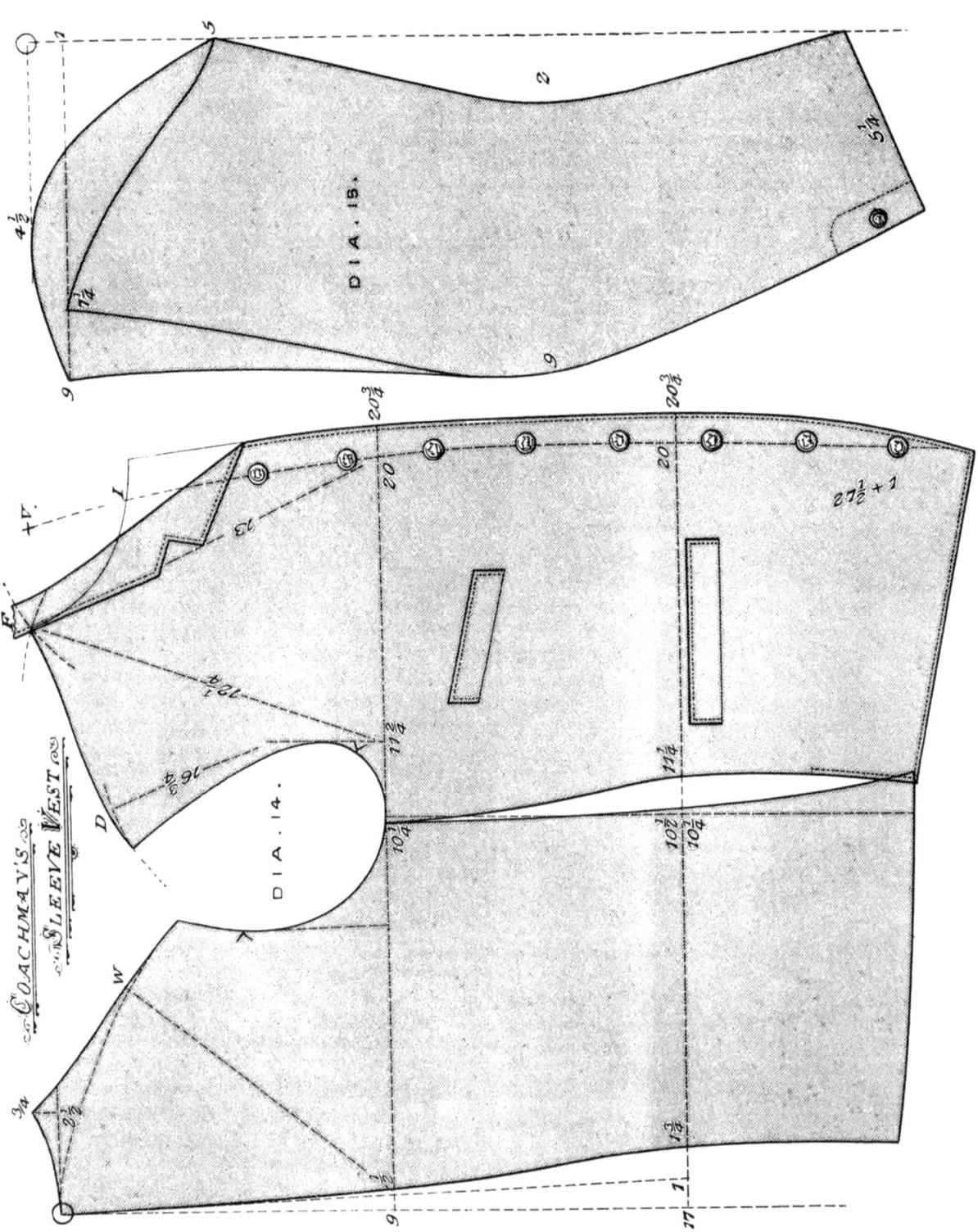

54

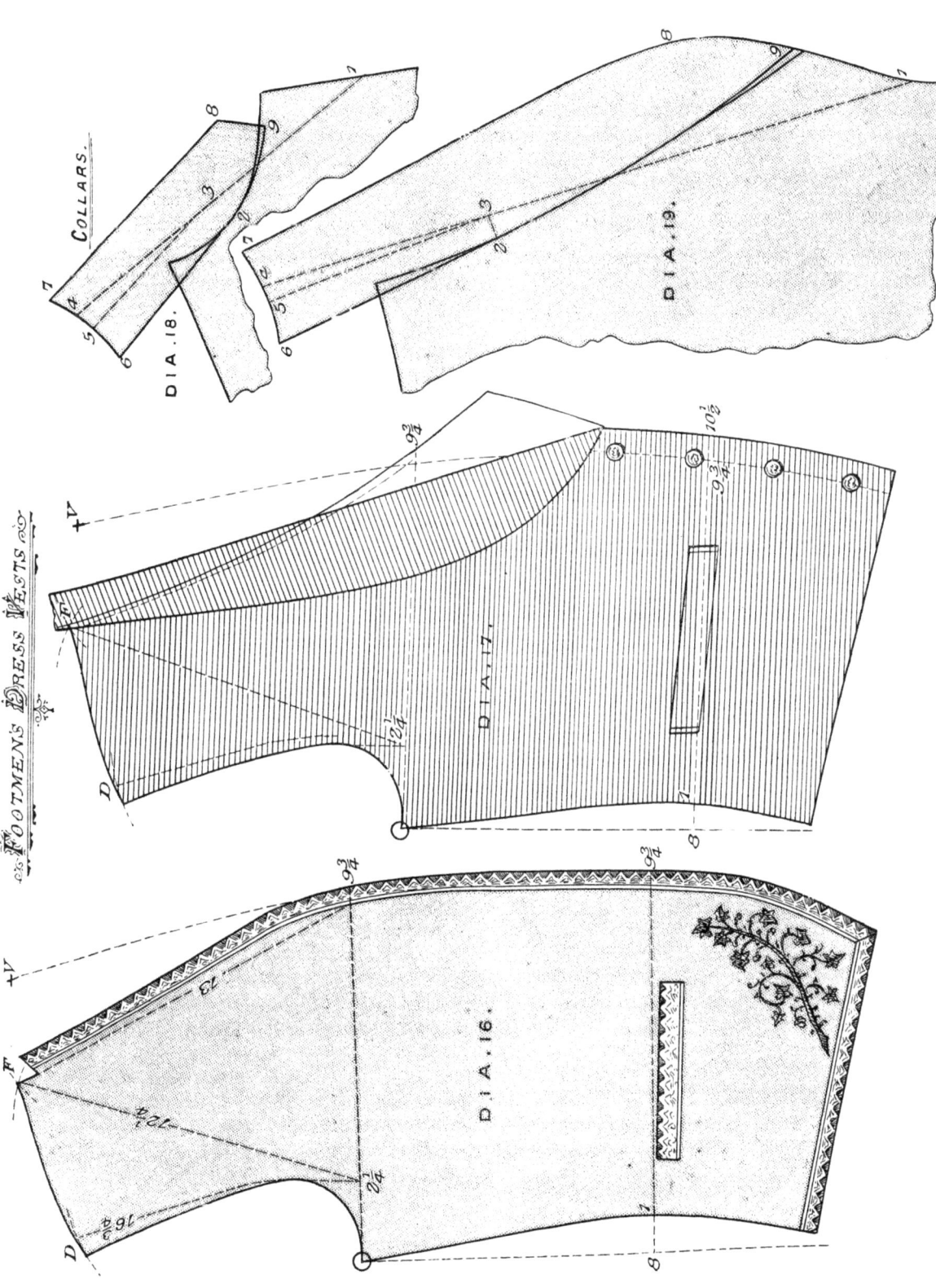

Plate 7.

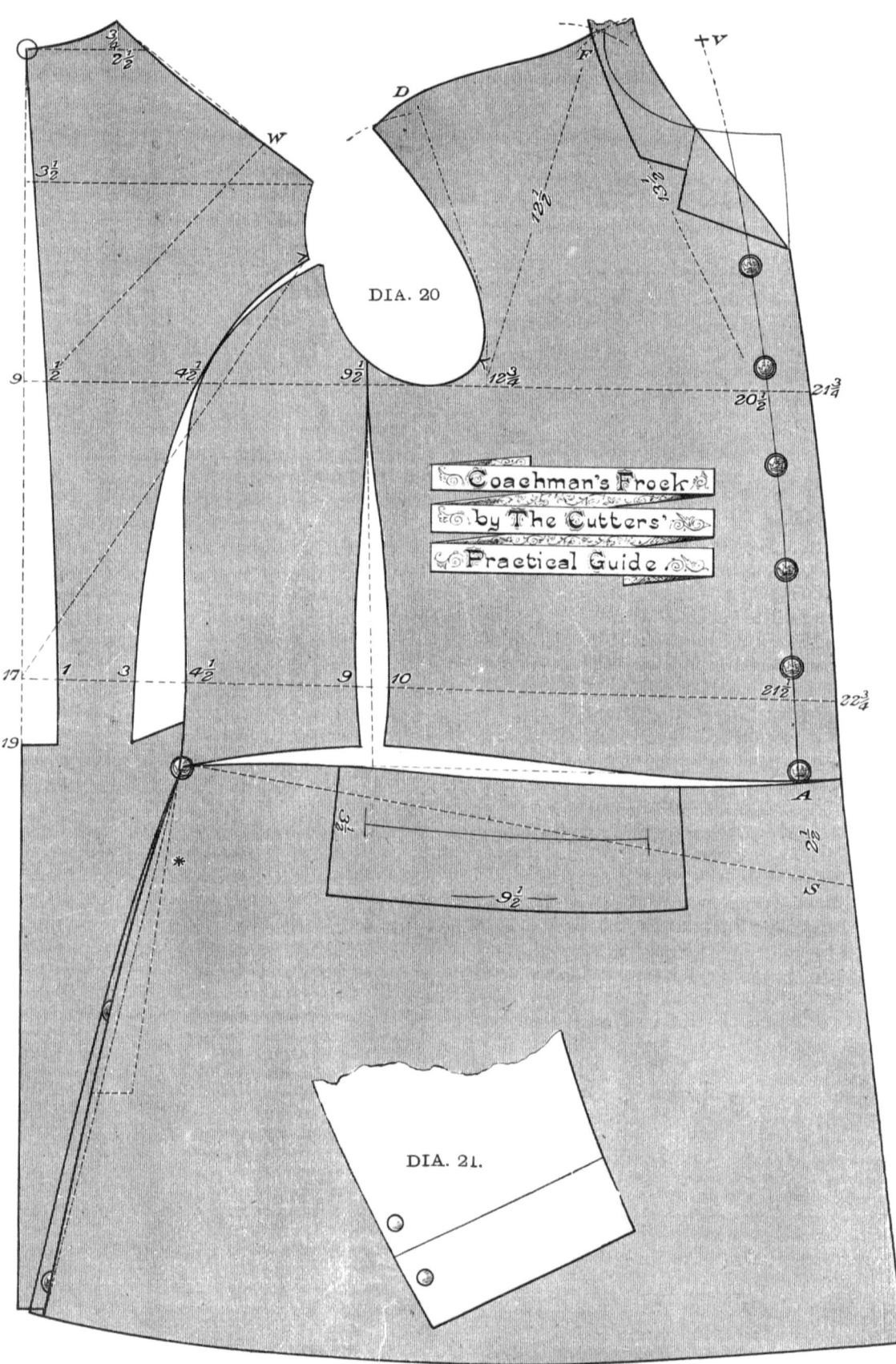

DIA. 20

Coachman's Frock
by The Cutters'
Practical Guide

DIA. 21.

Plate 8.

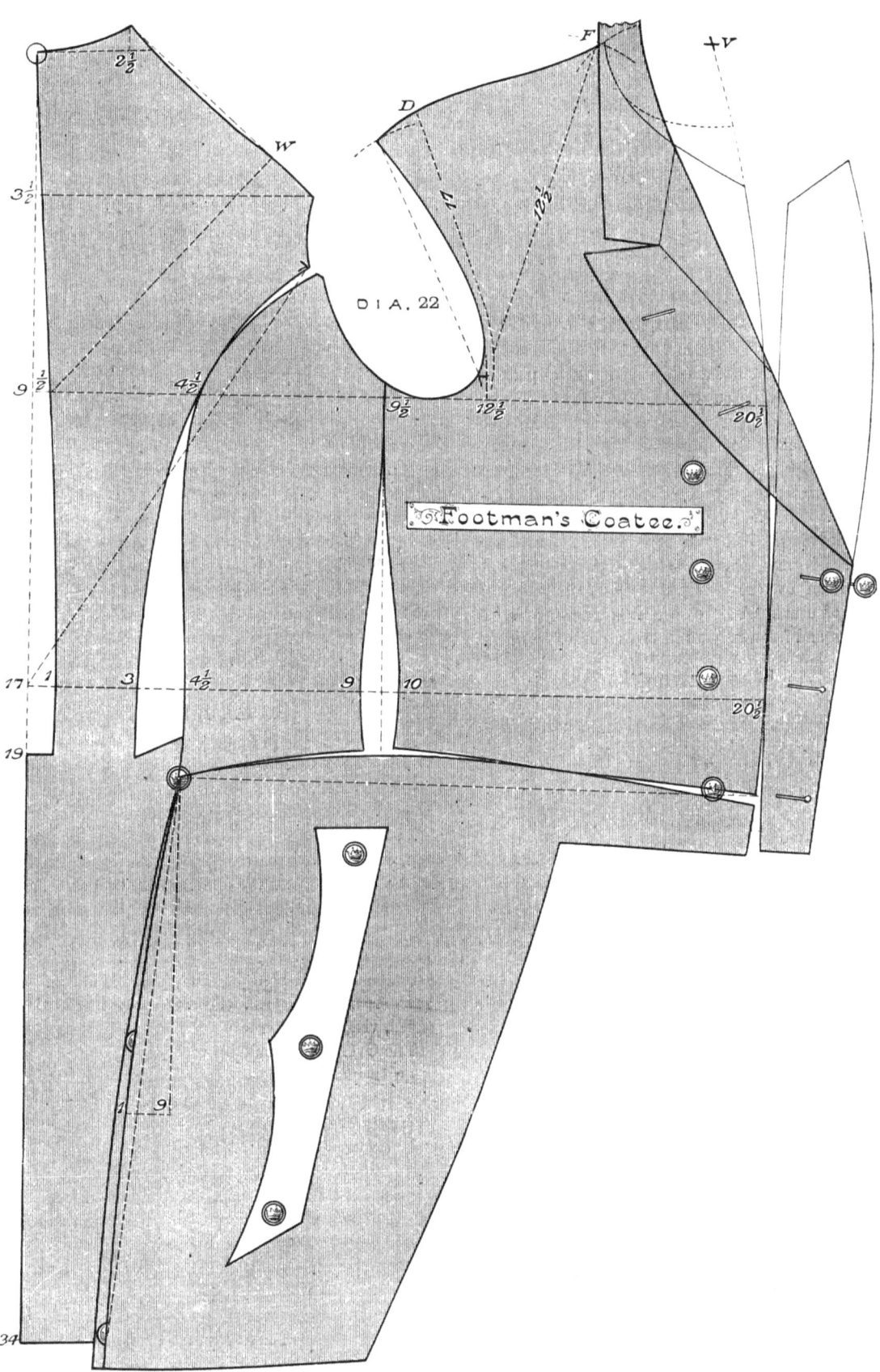

Footman's Coatee.

DIA. 22

Plate 9.

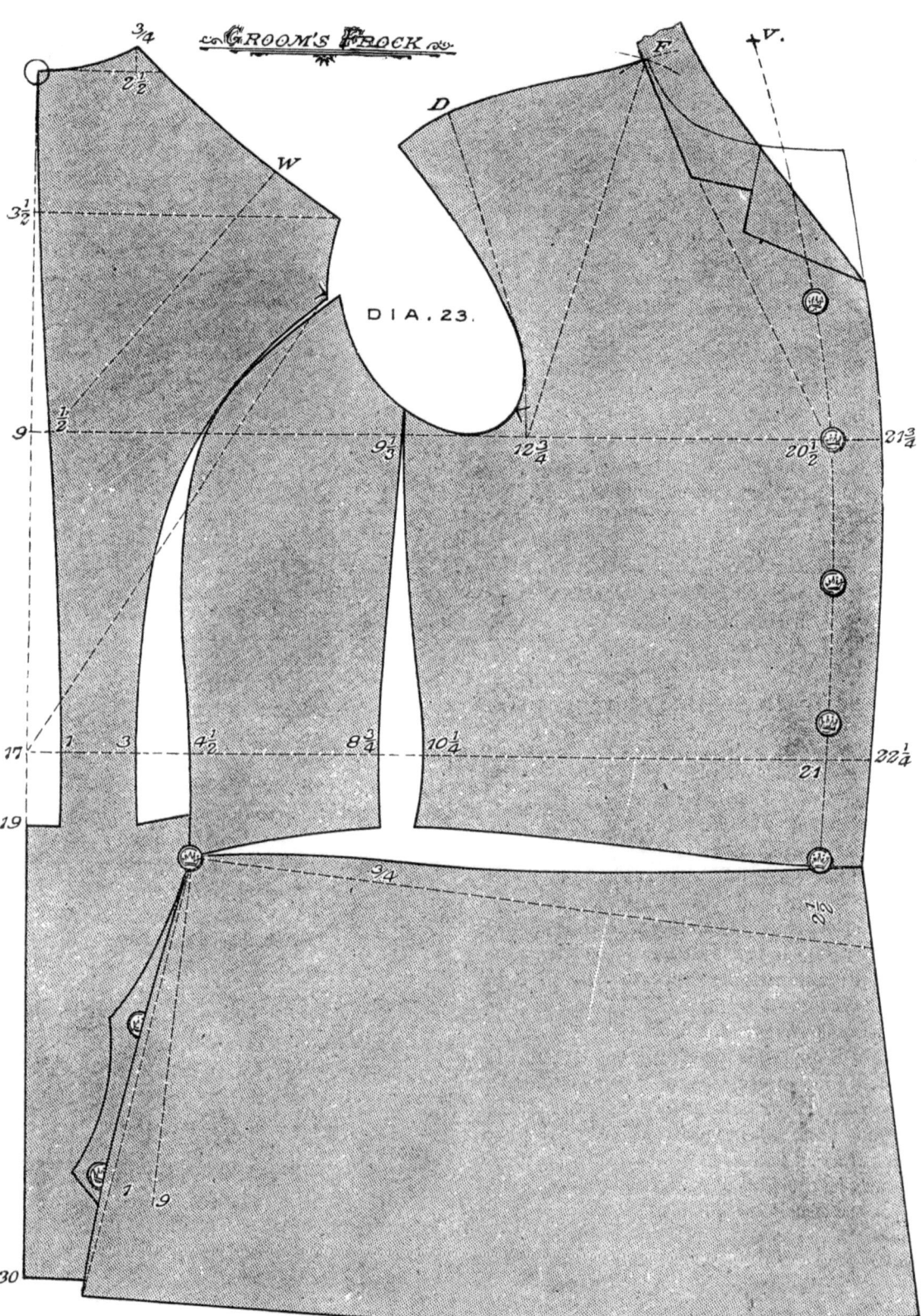

GROOM'S FROCK

DIA. 23.

Plate 10.

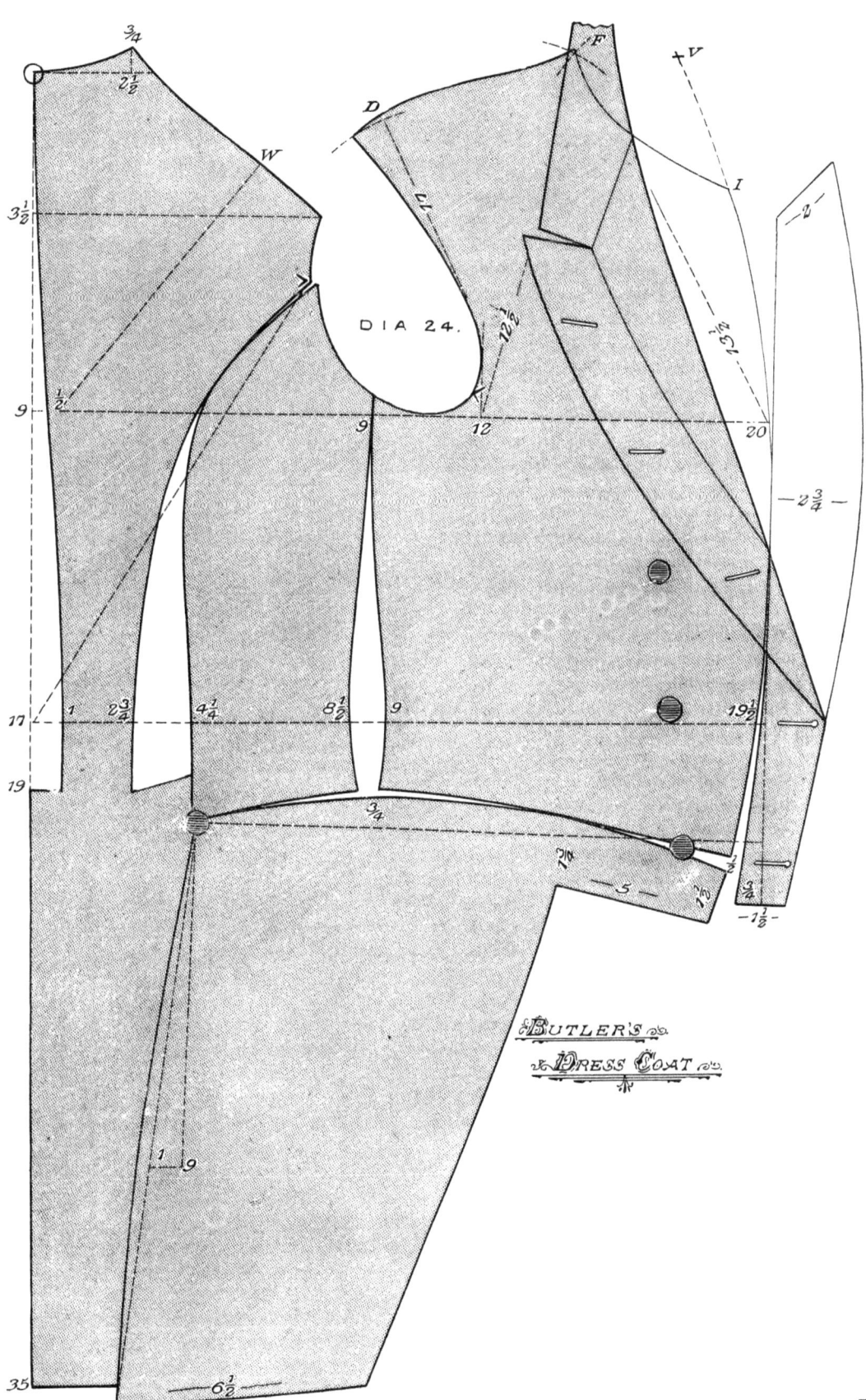

BUTLER'S
DRESS COAT

Plate 11.

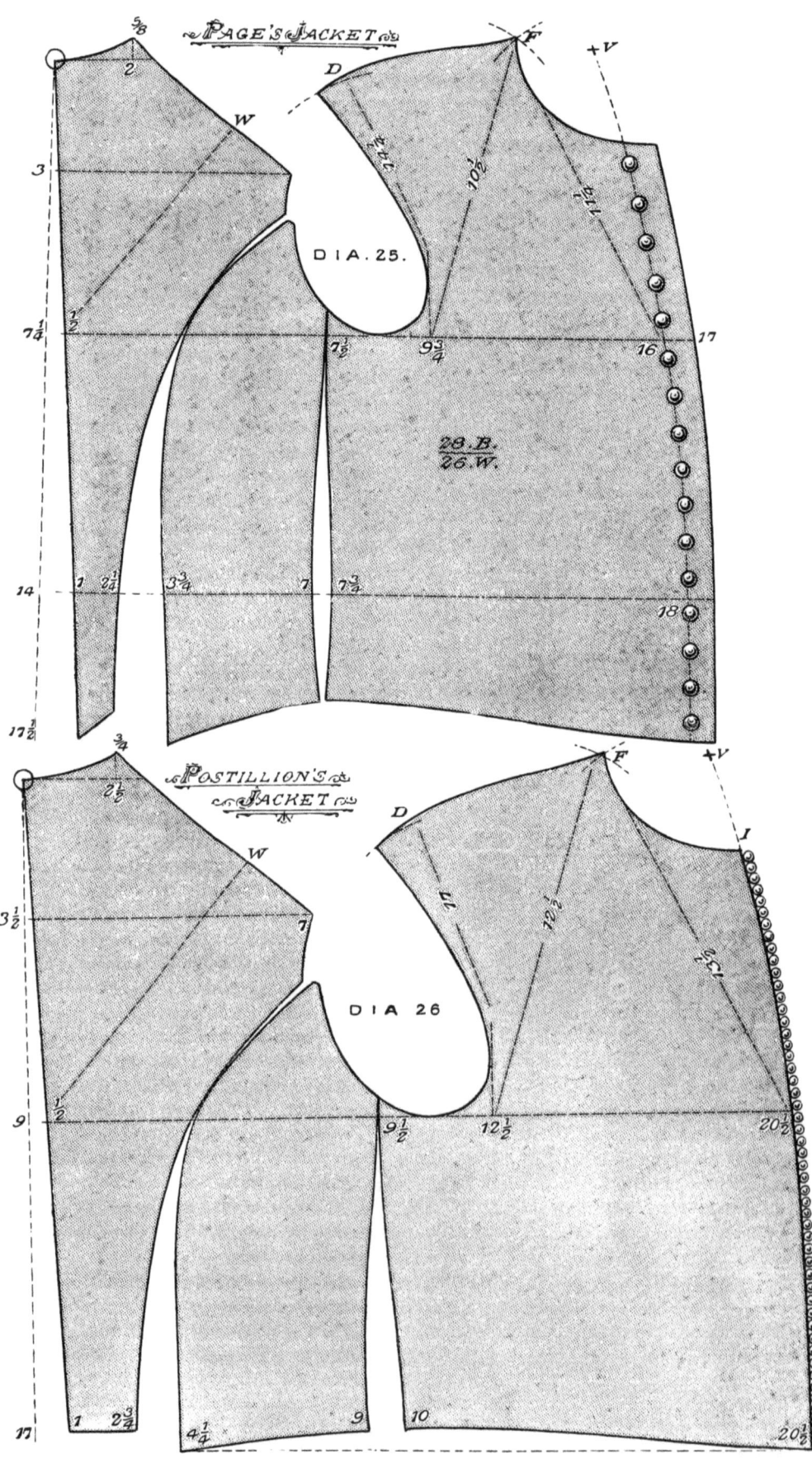

PAGE'S JACKET

DIA. 25.

28.B.
26.W.

POSTILLION'S JACKET

DIA 26.

Plate 12.

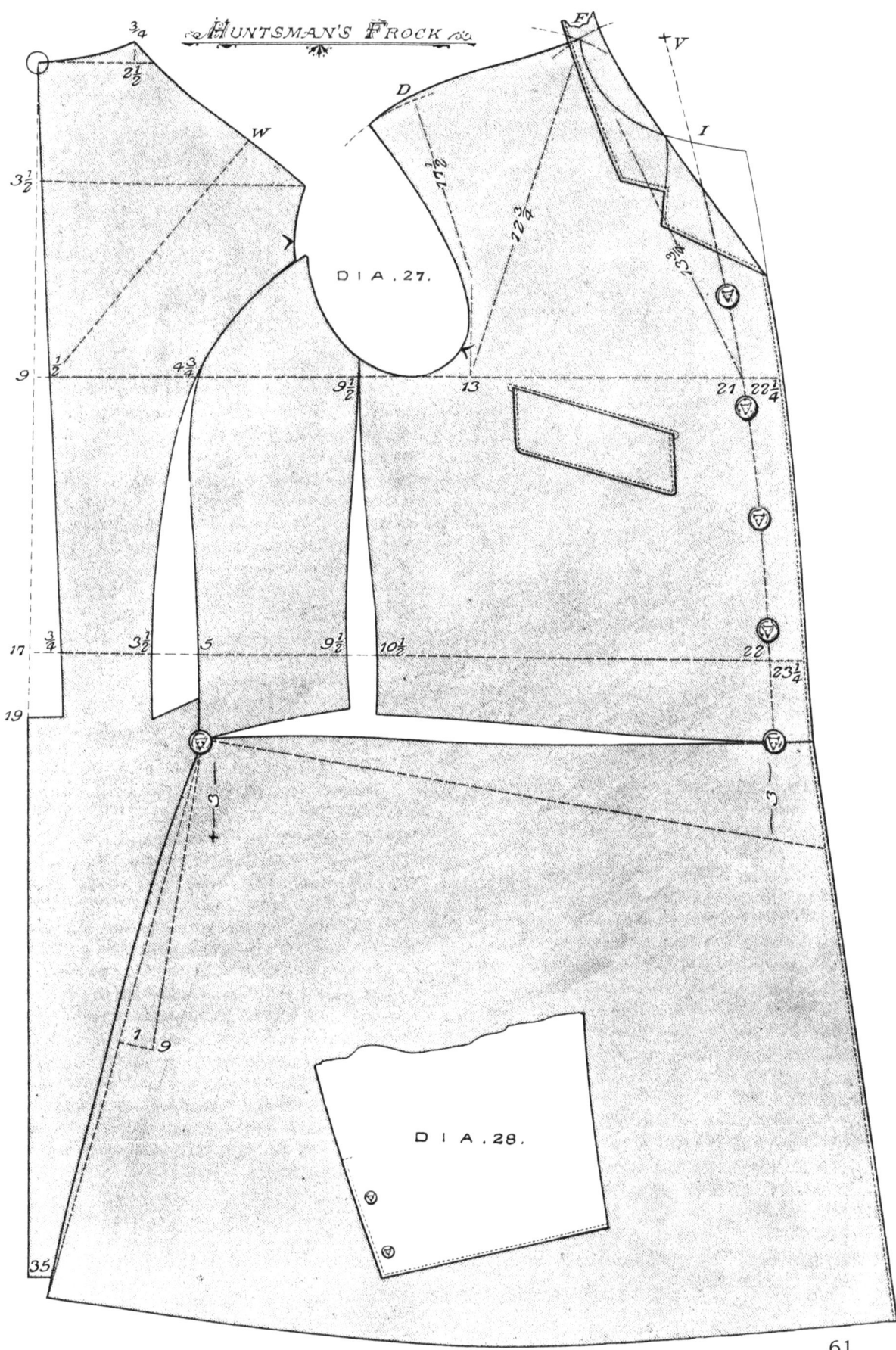

61

Plate 13.

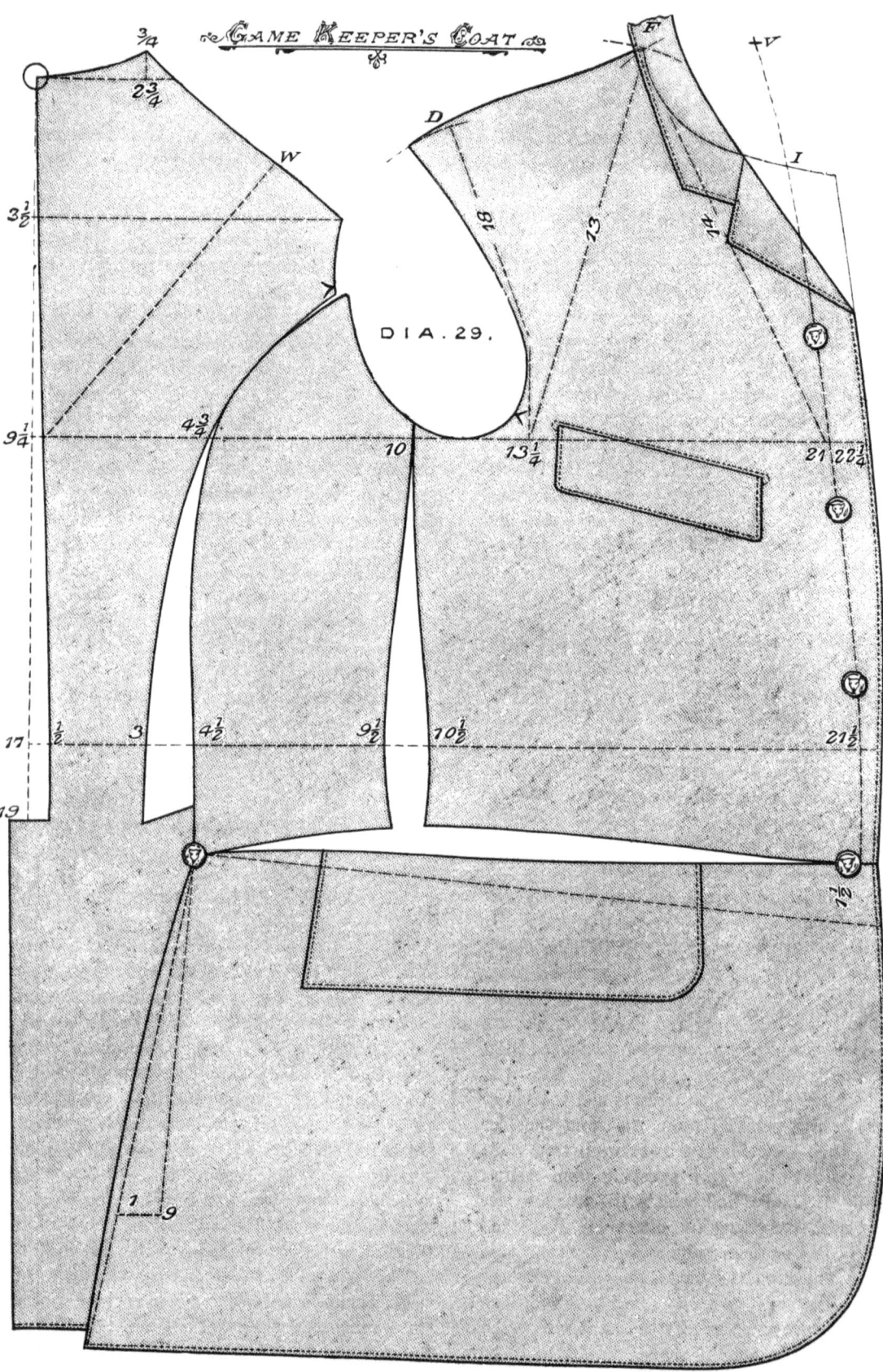

GAME KEEPER'S COAT

DIA. 29.

Plate 14.

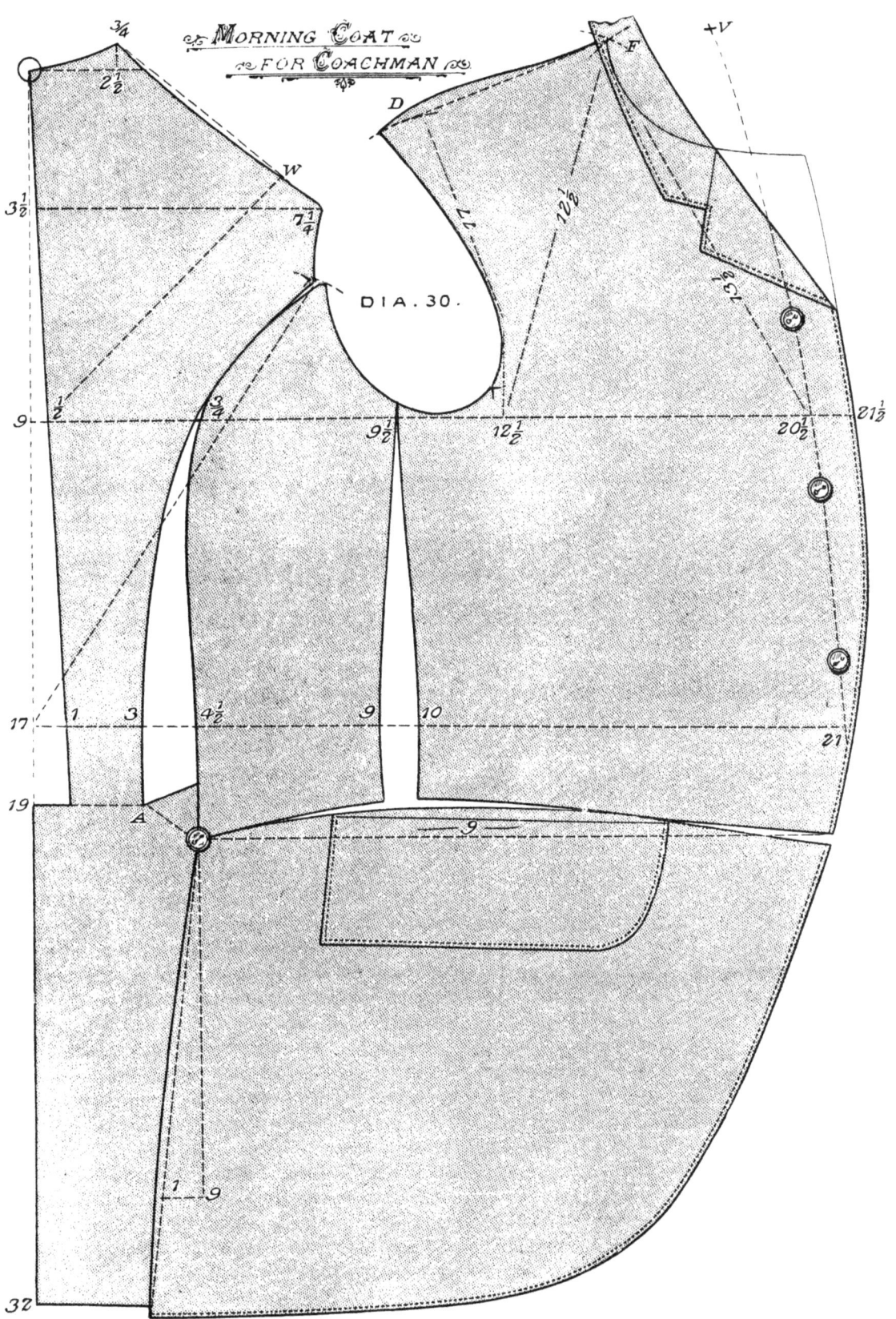

MORNING COAT
FOR COACHMAN

DIA. 30.

Plate 15.

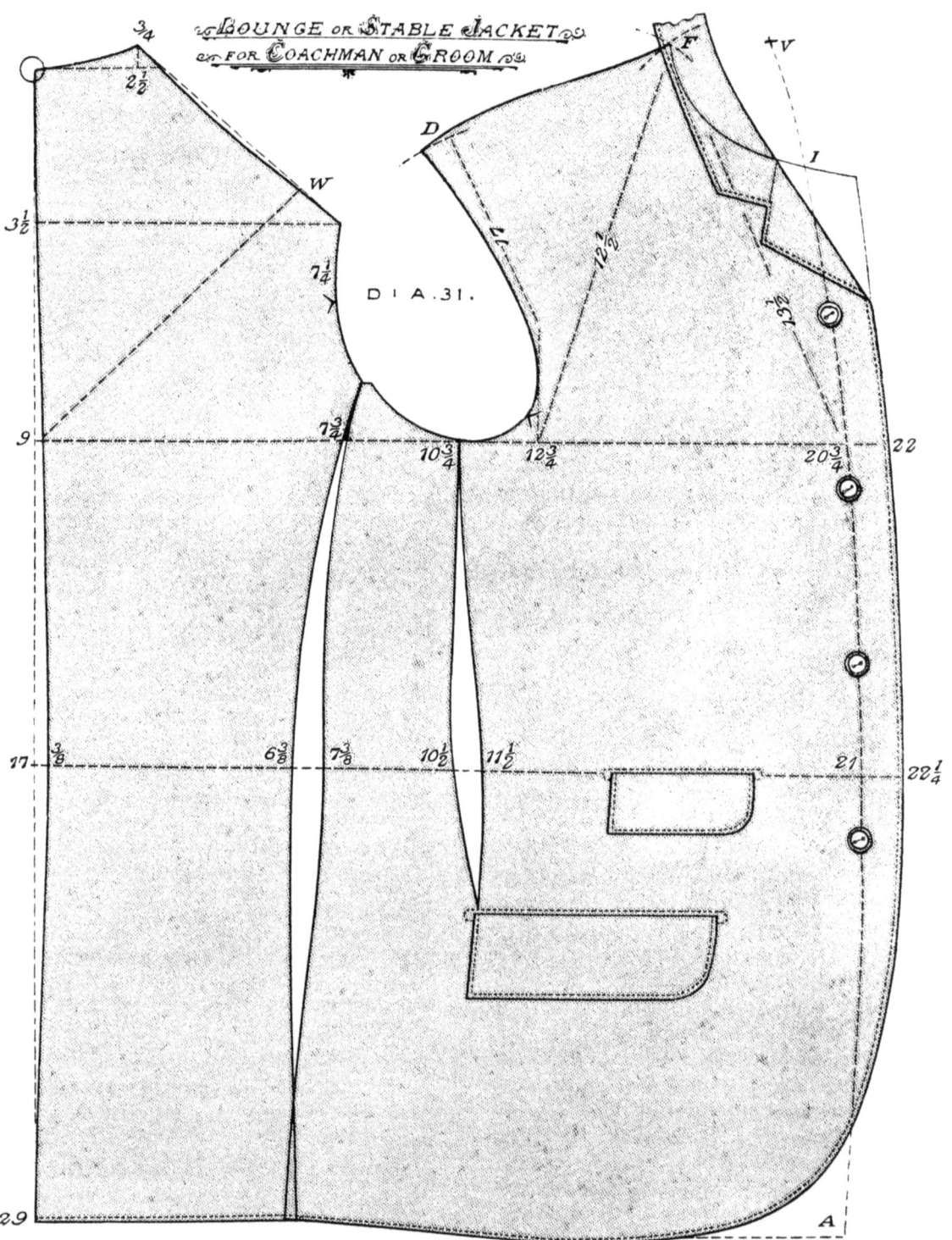

LOUNGE OR STABLE JACKET
FOR COACHMAN OR GROOM

DIA. 31.

Plate 16.

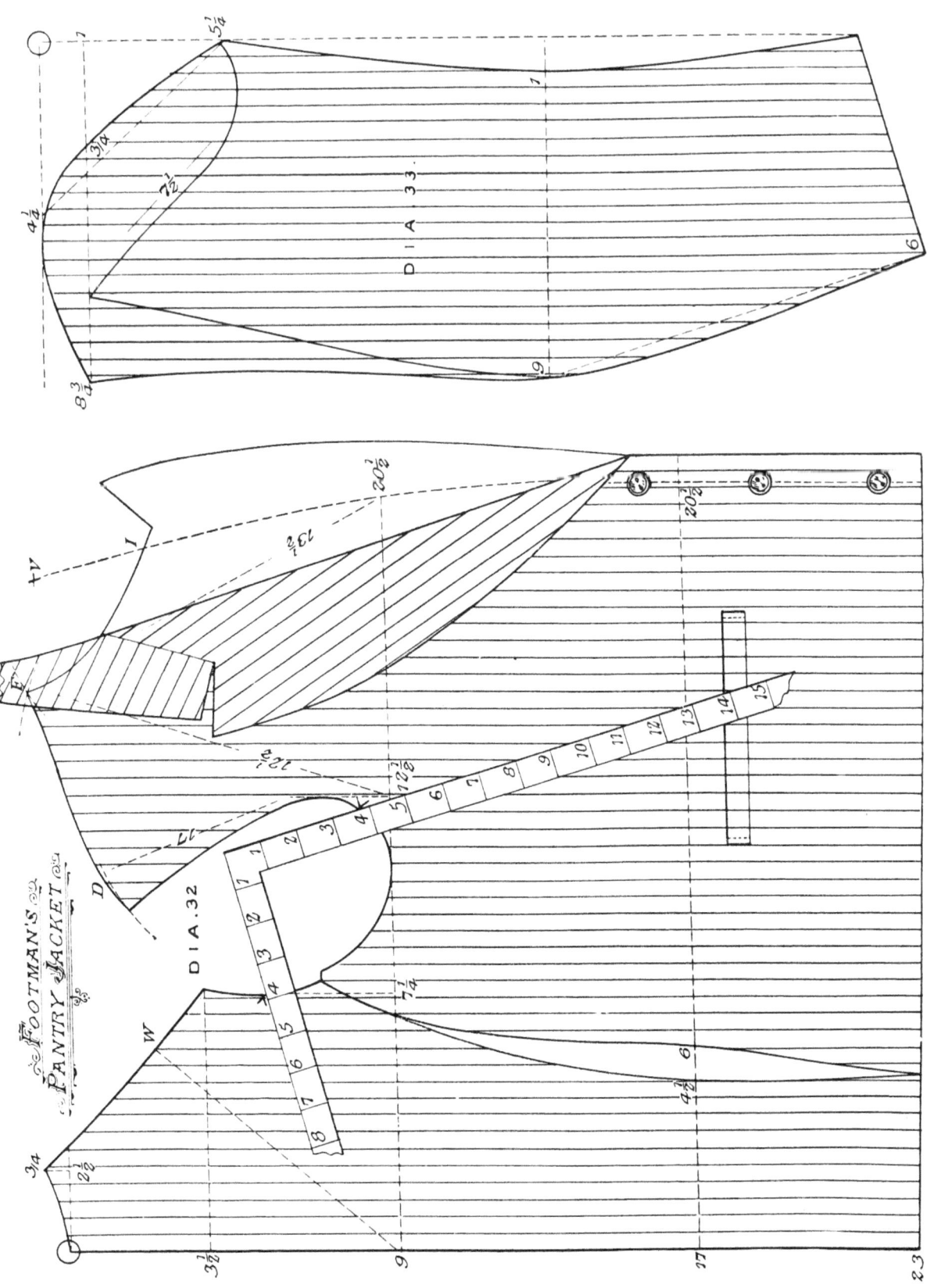

Plate 17.

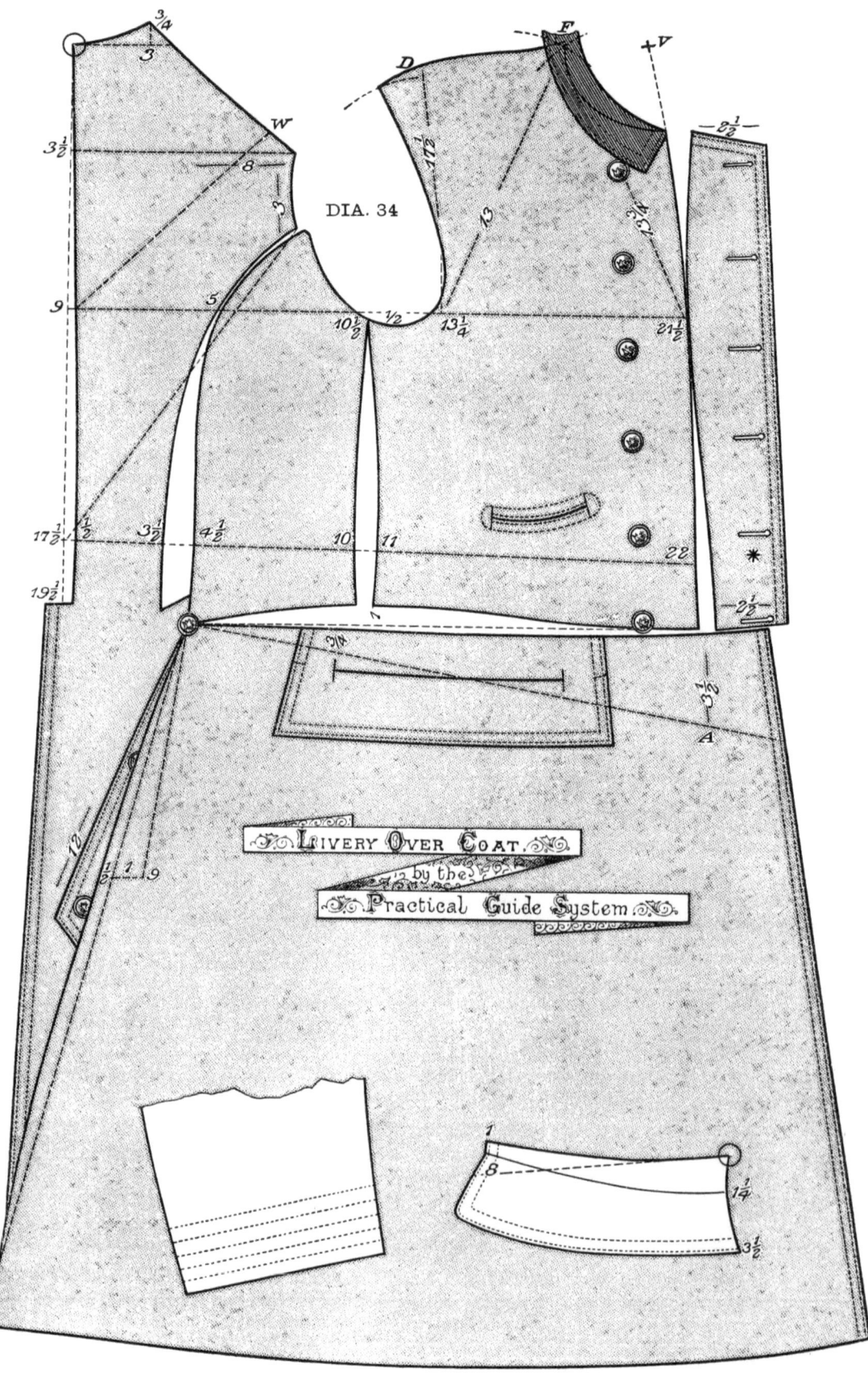

DIA. 34

LIVERY OVER COAT by the Practical Guide System

Plate 18.

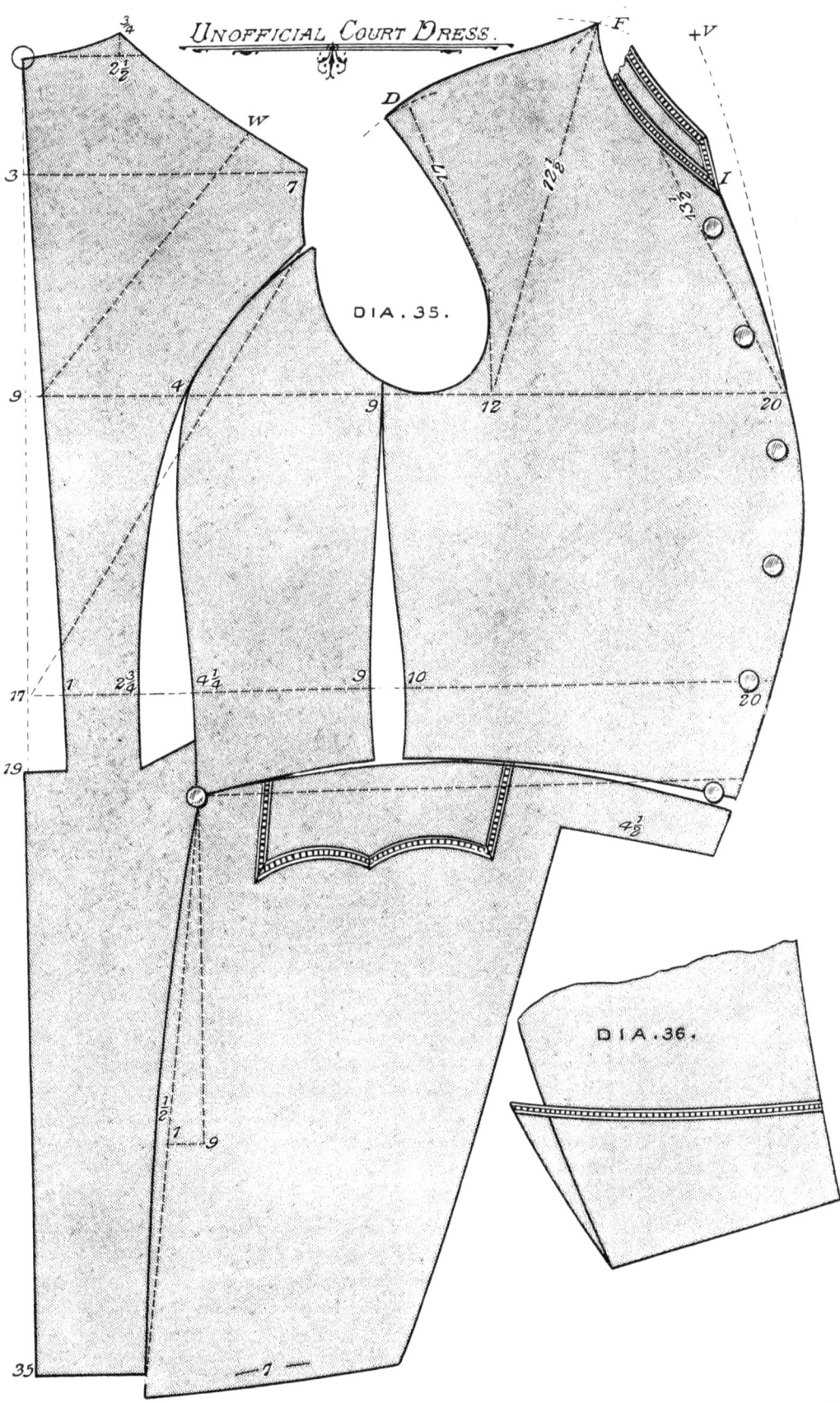

UNOFFICIAL COURT DRESS.

DIA. 35.

DIA. 36.

Plate 19.

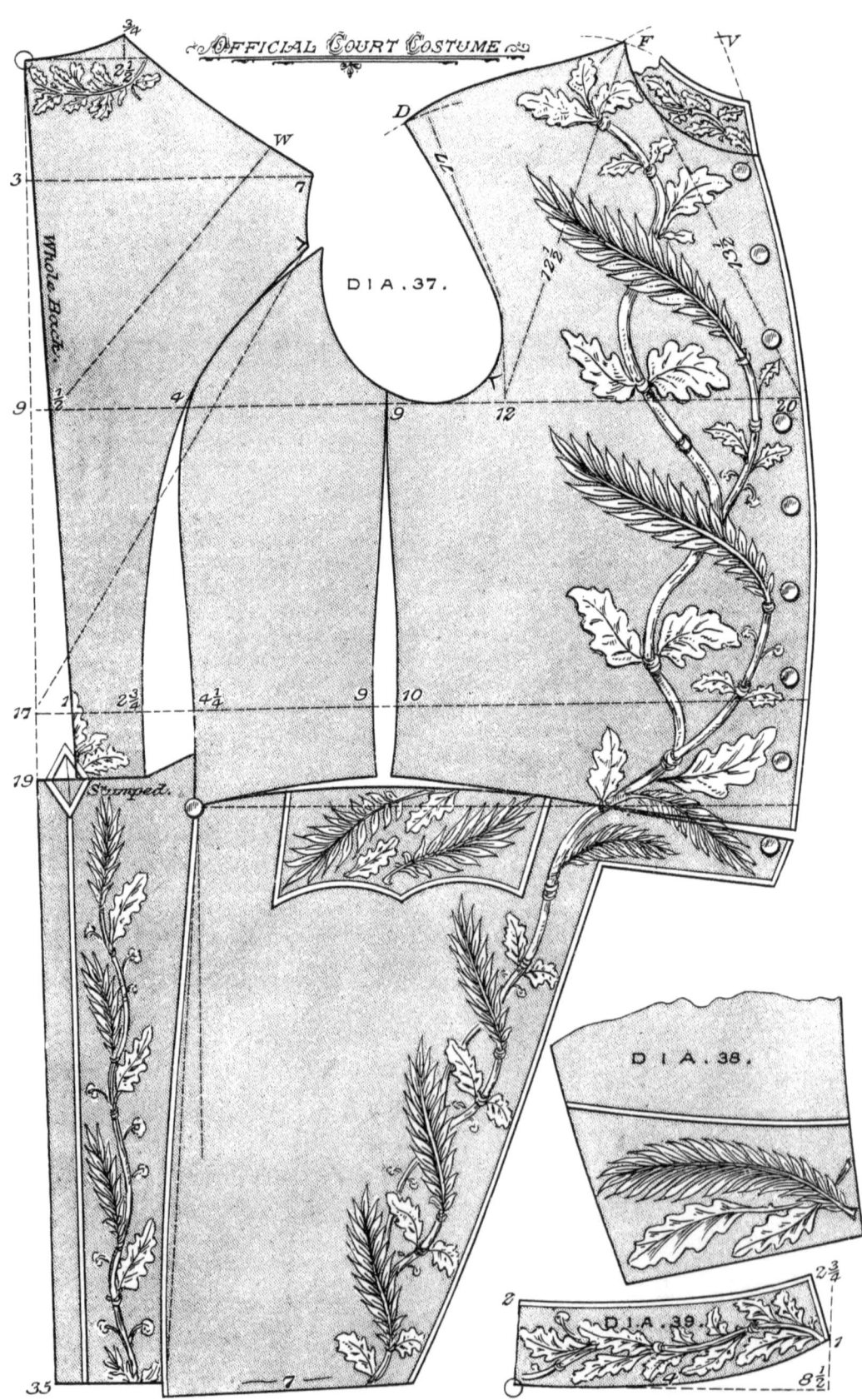

OFFICIAL COURT COSTUME

DIA. 37.

DIA. 38.

DIA. 39.

Whole Back

Stamped.

Plate 20.

Plate 21.

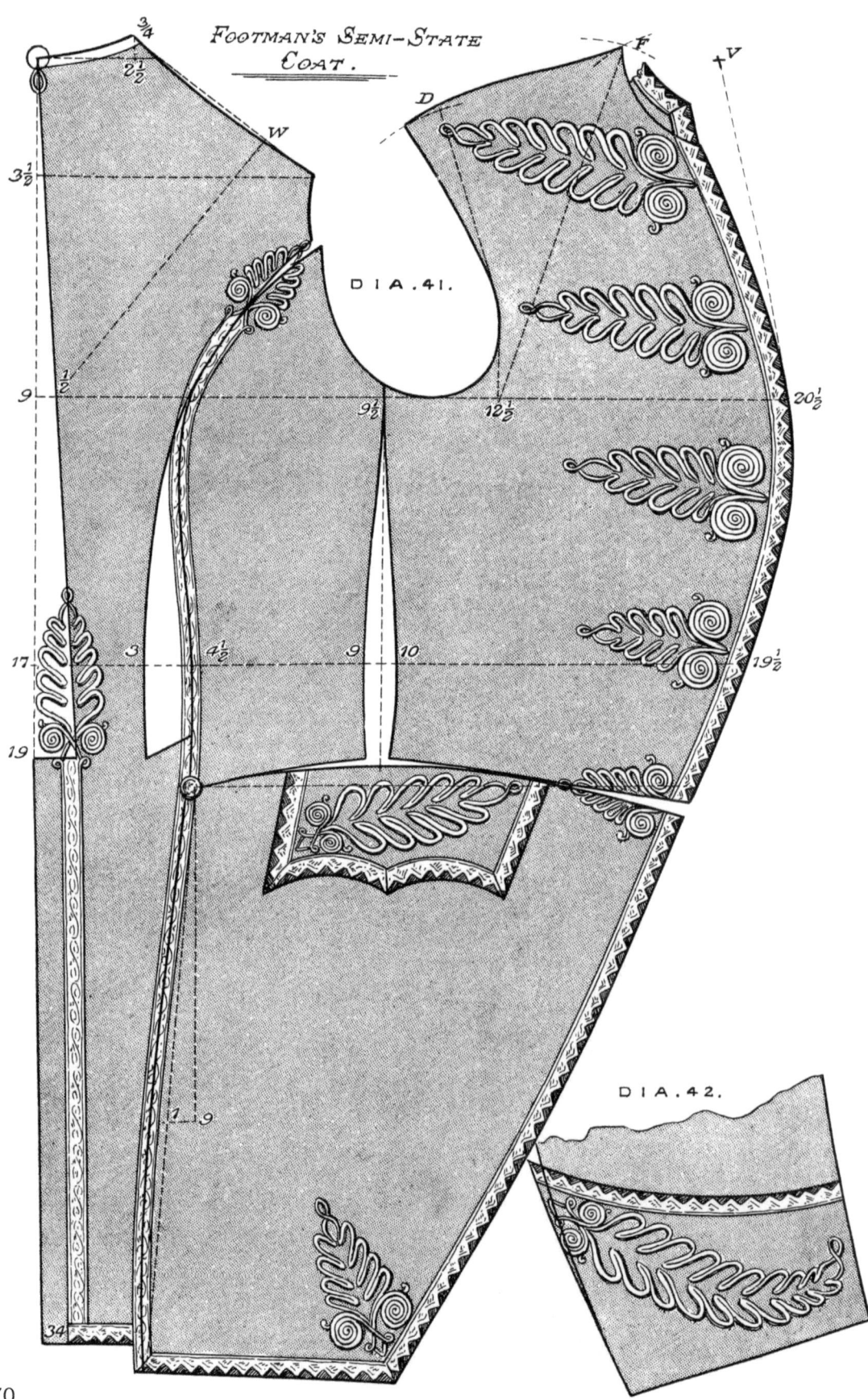

FOOTMAN'S SEMI-STATE
COAT.

DIA. 41.

DIA. 42.

Plate 22.

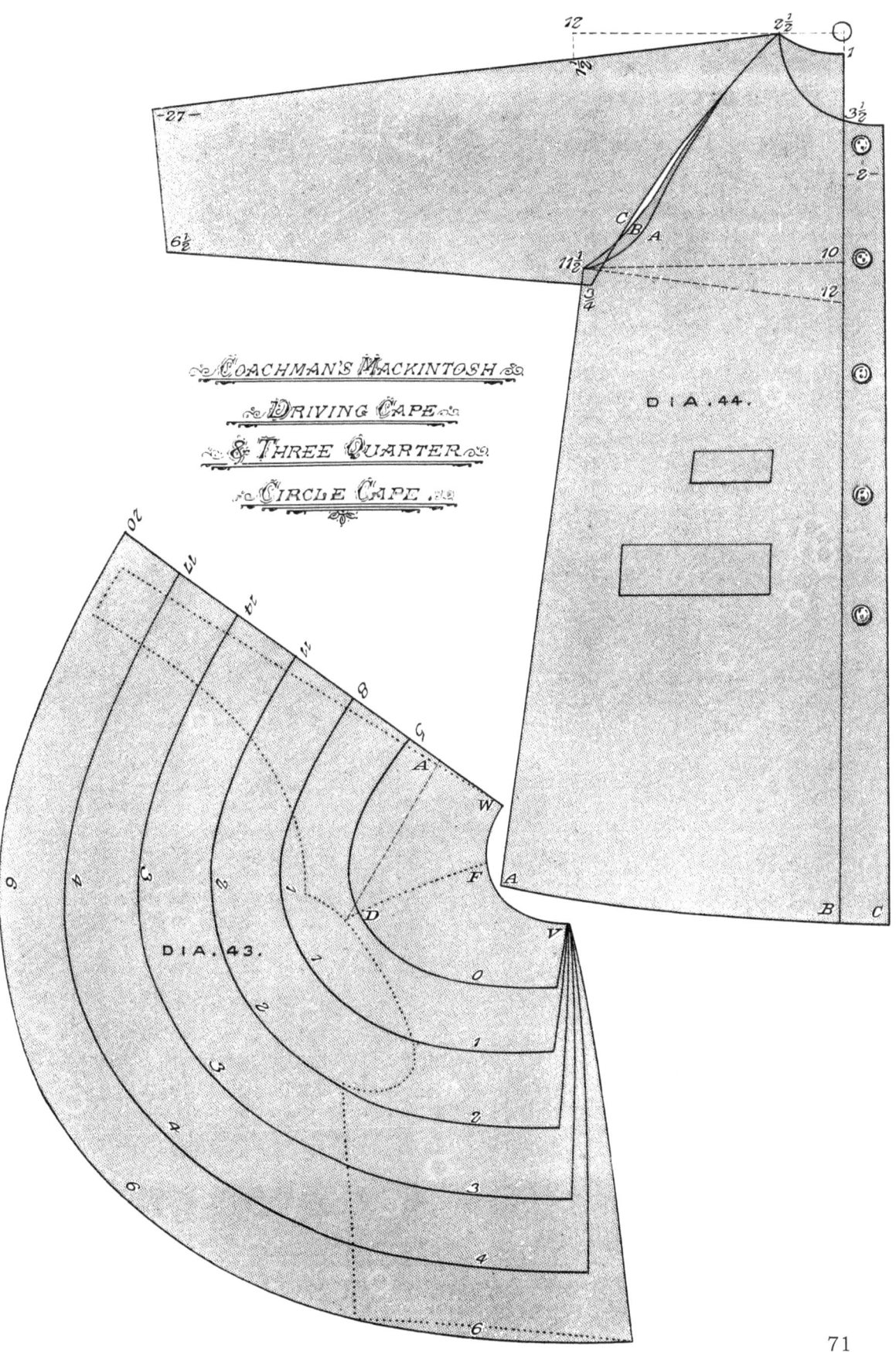

COACHMAN'S MACKINTOSH
DRIVING CAPE
& THREE QUARTER
CIRCLE CAPE.

DIA.44.

DIA.43.

Plate 23.

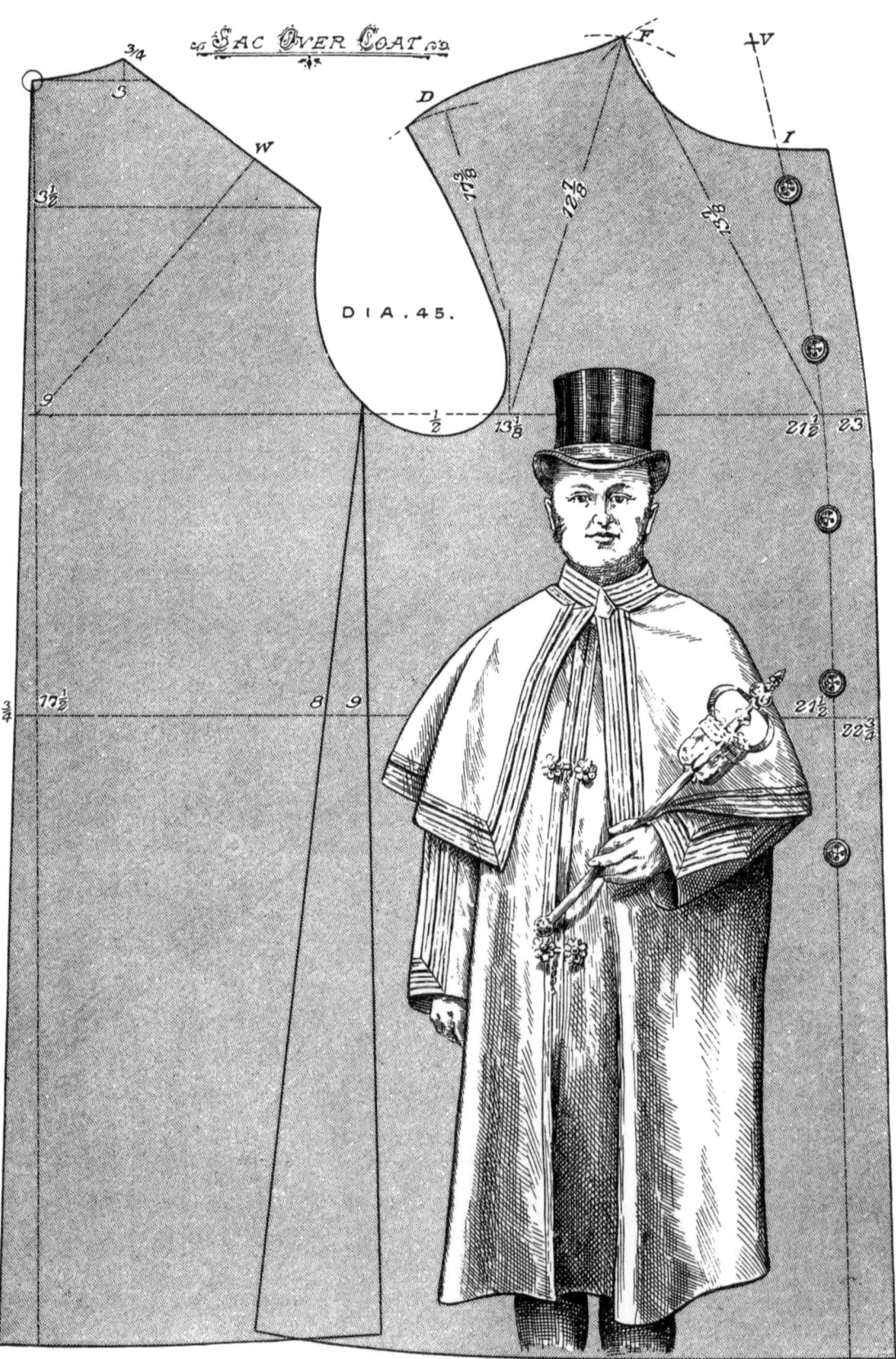

SAC OVER COAT

DIA. 45.

Plate 24.

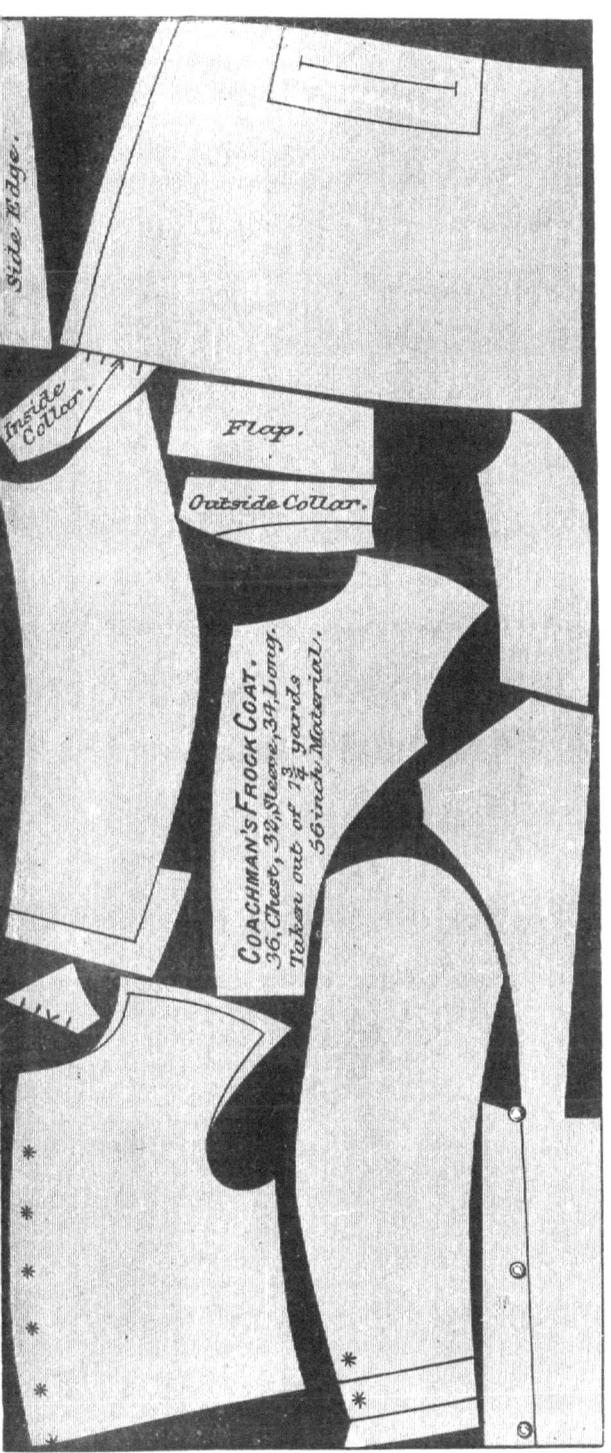

ECONOMY LAYS

For Coachman's Frock.   Footman's Coatee.

Plate 25.

Postillion's Full Dress Cap
and Wig.

Back view of Postillion's
Full Dress Jacket and Wig.

Front view of Postillion's
Full Dress Jacket with sham Vest.

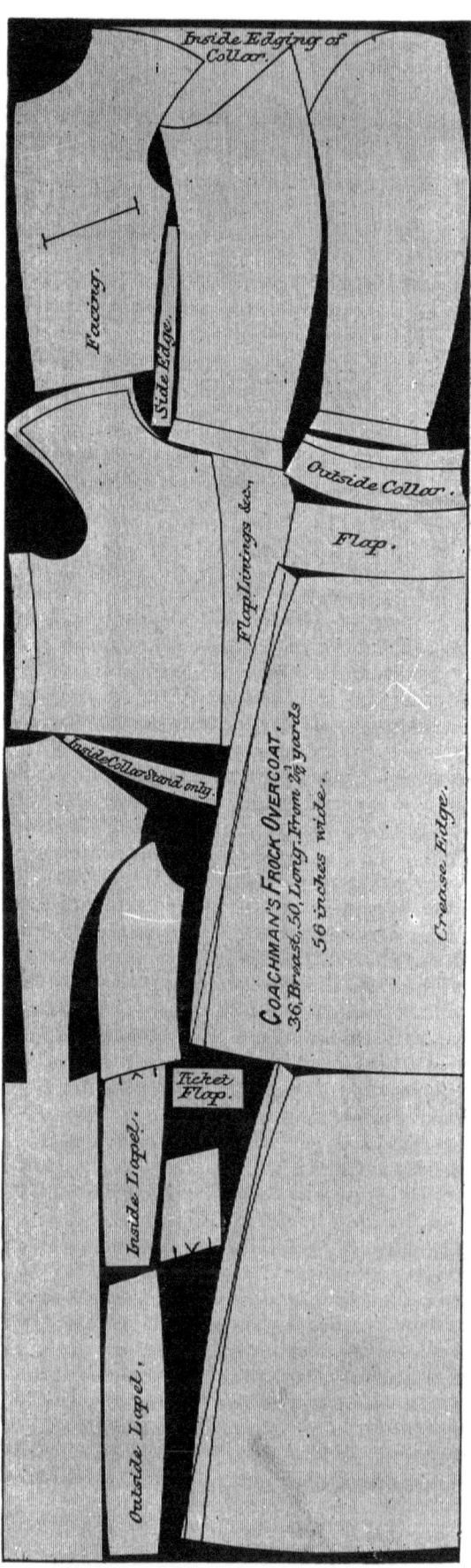

Economy Lay of Livery Overcoat.

APPENDIX

In arranging the matter and Plates facing each other, it has been found difficult to get all that should be said on some of the subjects into the space available, and in order that these items should not be omitted from the work we have arranged them under the above title.

Coachman's Riding Trousers
Diagram 2. Plate 1.

Coachman's Trousers vary from Footmen's in that they are generally made smaller in the legs, more open in the cut, and rather more seat angle. They form part of his stable Suit, and as they are often used for riding purposes it will be necessary for the cutter to find out whether he wants them to ride in *occasionally* or are they to be Riding Trousers proper. It is very necessary to find this out, as in Riding Trousers proper there is a considerable amount of fulness at the fork and generally provision for the position of the wearer on horseback. The principle employed, however, is the same, and consists in marking up from E to Y $\frac{1}{12}$ seat, and down from E to ? 9 inches, and going out from ? to R an amount varying with the style of Trousers desired: for those to ride in occasionally say ½ an inch, for a more open style of cut 1 inch, and for Riding Trousers proper 1½ inches is the correct amount. Line D C F is squared by line Y Z, and all the upper part of the Trousers is worked from lines squared from it, the quantities being found in the same way as for Diagram 1. The width of the leg is distributed on either side of centre line E L O, and in measuring the length of leg and position of the knee, measure from E to L and E to O, and square lines from this

point; this will give the extra length of leg necessary for the open style of cut beyond what he measure would indicate. The topsides should be 1 inch longer than leg measure from E to O, so that there may be an amount of fulness over the knee at M and N. The undersides in like manner have an inch extra length put at top of sideseam also for fulling over the seat at U, and in addition to this the amount of seat angle is increased from D to S by about the same quantity more than the usual $\frac{1}{12}$ seat as the legs are opened; for instance, if the legs were opened 1½ inches, the seat angle for a 36 seat would be 4½ inches, viz., one-twelfth seat plus 1½ inches. The smallness of the bottoms of these trousers necessitates the bottoms being much more hollow on the topsides and rounder on the undersides. The top of the forepart should be slightly lowered at H for Riding Trousers.

Piping the Sideseam of Trousers.

This operation requires a considerable amount of care. The first thing to do is to *tear* the strip of coloured cloth off the desired width, remembering that it must be double the width, allowing for the two seams and the width of piping desired; then baste it on level with the edge, and after that carefully baste the top and undersides together when it is ready for seaming which should be done very regularly, as the least variation shows in the width of piping. The seam should not be opened but pressed on one side as for a raised seam. We have sometimes seen them stitched on to the topside, then turned over the desired width of the piping and the topside stitched to the underside from

the outside, but this has the great objection for Livery that there is the row of stitching,which is inconsistent with the general plainness of Liveries. To inexperienced
hands this is doubtless the easier plan.

Position of Brace Buttons.

The front brace button should be ½ an inch nearer I, Diagram 1, than half-way from I to H, and the other one 3½ inches nearer I. The back brace button should not be more than 2 inches from seat seam. The position of the fly buttons should be arranged so that the edge of fly just covers the seam of the catch.

The Position of Strap Buttons.

To find the position of the strap buttons at the bottom of Riding Trousers, come in from O to X, Diagram 2, 1 inch, and mark on either side of that from 3½ to 4 inches, or equal to half the distance from edge of heel on side to edge of heel on the leg plus ½ an inch. This will find the position of the first strap button; the other one, if there is a second, would be placed in front of this. Linen should be put inside the inlay, which should be firmly tacked through the outside, though the sewing on the buttons must not show through, As there is a considerable strain on these, they should be sewn on securely.

Hints on the Making-up of Breeches.

Making has so much to do with success in Breeches that we give a few hints on that important operation. The undersides should be carefully shrunk under the knee, and the topsides well fulled on at both side and legseams at the same part; the amount of fulness should not be less than 1 inch, and

this can be easier and more correctly distributed by putting in a drawing thread, drawing it in the necessary amount, and pressing the fulness away before the seams are sewn. This method is much better than the ordinary fulling on and shrinking after the seams are sewn, as it ensures the fulness being correctly located as well as being nicely worked away.

The undersides should be fulled on over the seat in the same way. The knee, small, and calf, should be made up to button just to the measure or a trifle less, as a tight-fitting knee is essential in all breeches. The buttons should be sewn on strongly, and a good neck given them to facilitate the buttoning. The calf button should be put just on the centre of calf, so that the buttons of Breeches and Gaiters will harmonize and show two buttons above the top of the Gaiters. The tack is placed 1 inch below the keee, and the top button 1 inch below the tack. If strapping is put on the legseams, it is placed about 2½ or 3 inches on either side of the legseam, and usually extends to half-way up from knee to fork, occasionally higher.

To Cut Whole-falls.

Proceed with the foreparts as for fly fronts, and reduce the top as from 2 to 6 and 1 to 5 about 2 inches, taking care to leave a little round on at 5 so as to avoid any hollow when the fall seam is sewn. To cut the bearer, place the topsides down and continue up from 6 to 2 the amount the topsides have been reduced in length, and continue down to 3 not less 5 inches; mark across the top from 2 to 1, and mark 1 4 ¾ of an inch beyond the fall seam; 4 should be 3 or 3½ inches below 5, and complete the bottom of bearer as illustrated. We would especially caution our readers against getting them too shallow at 5.

In making up, the pockets are inserted in the bearer in about the position marked, a facing is put to take the holes and buttons, and the bearer is completed by waistband or lining as usual with fly fronts. A facing should be put across the fall, preferably of the same material, but if this is not available, then Silesia or a similar material may be used.

Bilston Bearers

The alteration for Bilston Bearers is shown by the dot and dash line; the bearer as will be seen, is cut much deeper — 9 or 10 inches from top to bottom is the usual depth of the Bilston Bearer — the facing of the fall being brought down to it and the facing and bearer are then sewn together, making the seam preferably a little round. As will be seen, this style is a little lower at the side, say 6½ from D. If lined, as these generally are, the pockets would then be inside as much as if they were fly fronts, a neat finish being thus obtained. The bearer is turned in at the curved part below C and the lining felled on to it down to the corner, across the fall facing and then up on the other side; the top part of the bearer, as from C to A L E, is generally bound. The sewing of the bearer to the fall facing requires a little care, it is done almost the last thing; when all the buttons are sewn on they are buttoned up, and then the true lay can be got, when the fall and bearer are firmly baisted together and then the bottom edge is sewn previous to felling on the linings. It is necessary to fasten the lining very firmly at the bottom corner of bearer, as there is a strain at that part, and for this purpose they are stitched round by hand behind the felling, and after a buttonhole stitch used just at the corner in line of felling.

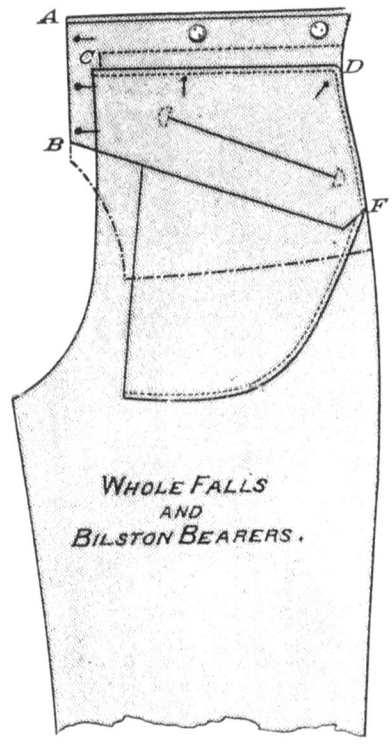

WHOLE FALLS
AND
BILSTON BEARERS.

**Split Falls.
See Plate 2.**

These are cut as follows: Complete draft as for fly fronts and cut off 1 inch right across top. Now mark position of split at 8 10, making 8 about 2 inches from 7 and 10 about ½ or ¾ inch further from fall seam. The space between 8 and 3 is then cut out about 1 inch lower down; the part above line 2 3 is used to face the pocket-mouth; the top waist-band and pocket-bearer is cut as illustrated by 1, 2, 3, 4, 5, 6. The small bearer to fill in fall is outlined by 7, 8, 9, 10; from 8 to 10 is from 6 to 7 inches. The dark shaded part is a welt which is put on to hide the seam at 8 10; at the top of this a hole is placed to fasten to a button put on the bearer, and the bottom is usually finished with a sprat's head or three-cornered tack. The pocket is of the frog-mouthed type, a sort of half side, half cross pocket, and gene-rally fastened with a hole and button at the corner. The distance from 6 to 5 is a matter of taste, but 3 to 5 should not be more than 6 inches.

VESTS.
Taking the Measures.

We have fully described how to take the measures for the various garments in Part 1 of "The Cutters' Practical Guide", but in order to make such Part complete in itself we will briefly explain the mode of measuring.

For Coats and Vests we advocate four extra measures being taken beyond those usually adopted, viz., depth of scye, across; chest, front shoulder, and over shoulder.

To take the depth, put the tape over the neck and pass it down the front of each arm and take it back under the bottom of armpit to the centre of back, Figure 2, point B, taking care that the tape is taken across the back in a line parallel with the floor. This may also be obtained by putting a square up to the bottom of the armpit, and when quite level making a mark on back and front, and then making another mark on centre of back quite level with the one made at back of arm.

The Depth of Scye

Measure is then taken from the nape of point A, Figure 2, to B of Figure 2.

The Across Chest Measure

Is taken from the front of one scye to the front of the other, taking the measure about the middle of arm at top, from E to E, Fig. 1.

The Front Shoulder Measure

Is taken from the nape of the neck, point A, Figure 2, to the level of the bottom of the armpit, point D, Figure 1.

The Over Shoulder Measure

is taken from point B, Figure 2, over the shoulder at C and down to point D, Figure 1.

The front shoulder and over shoulder measures should be taken rather tightly and the across chest measure rather easily. In applying these measures it is not necessary to allow for seams, as the ordinary making up allows for that.

The measures necessary for a Vest are chest, waist, opening, measuring from the nape to the opening, and the full length taken from nape to bottom of Vest; also the four measures described.

For Coats of all kinds the following is the order of taking the measures: chest, waist, depth of scye, natural waist (fashion waist for Body Coats), full length, width across back, continue to elbow and length desired, the across chest measure, the front shoulder and the over shoulder.

The depth of scye equals ¼ breast. The across chest equals ¼ breast minus 1 inch.

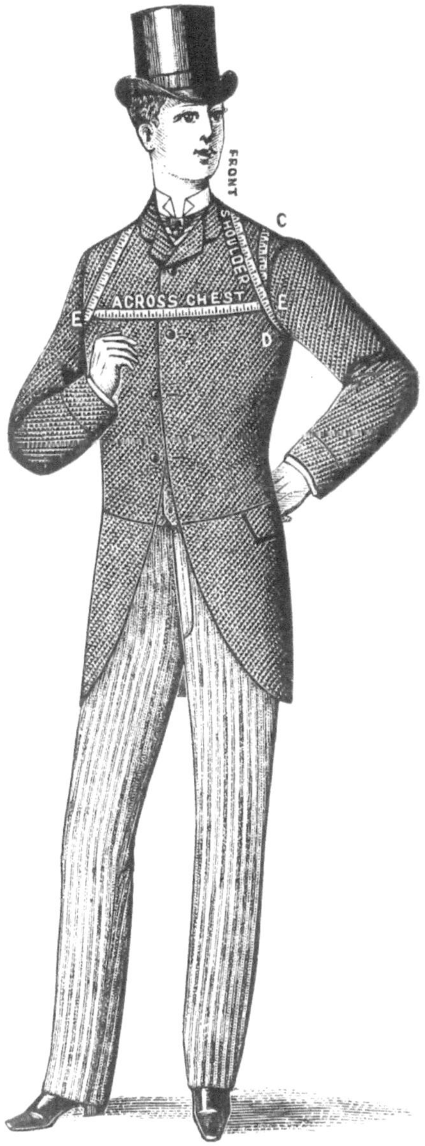

Fig. 1.

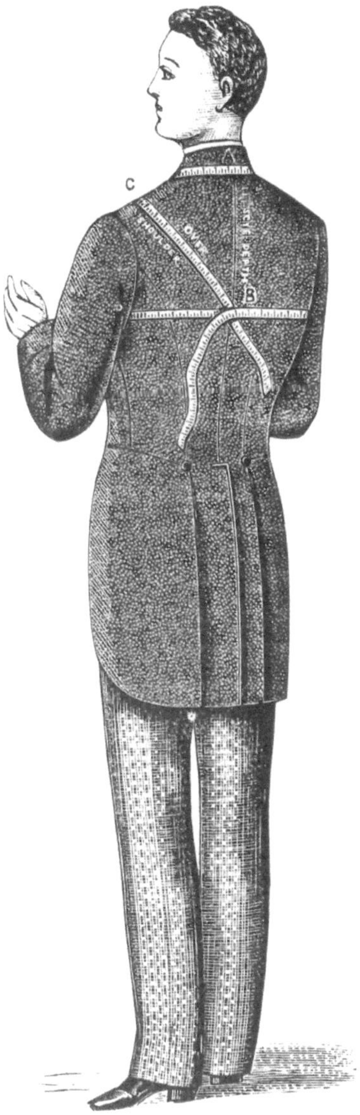

Fig 2.

TAKING THE MEASURES.

Chest	Waist	Scye Depth	Lounge. Nat. Waist	Lounge. Length	Morning Coat. Fas. Waist	Morning Coat. Length	Across Back	Full length sleeve	Across Chest	Front Shoulder	Over Shoulder
32	28	8¼	16	28	18	31½	6½	30	7¼	11½	15½
34	30	8⅝	16½	28½	18½	32	6⅞	31	7⅝	12	16¼
36	32	9	17	29	19	32½	7¼	32	8	12½	17
38	34	9⅜	17¼	29½	19¼	33	7⅝	33	8½	13	17¾
40	37	9¾	17¾	30	19¾	33½	8	33½	9	13½	18½
42	39½	10⅛	18	30½	20	34	8⅜	33½	9½	14	19¼
44	42	10½	18¼	31	20¼	34	8¾	34	10	14½	20
46	46	10¾	18½	31½	20½	34½	9	34	10½	15¼	21
48	50	11	18½	32	20½	34½	9¼	34	11	16	22
50	54	11¼	18½	32	20½	35	9½	34	11½	16¾	23

Scale of average measures to be used when the measures cannot be taken direct on the customer.

The front shoulder equals ⅓ breast plus ½ inch. The over shoulder equals ½ breast minus 1 inch. This for the proportionate figure of medium size. The annexed scale gives the average measures from 32 to 50 breast.

Variations in the location of the side-seam are often made in Vests, and the principle involved is to take from the one part and add the same amount to the other. Thus, if the material is short and you find it necessary to cut the forepart 1 inch narrower than usual, all that is necessary is to add on 1 inch to the side-seam of the back, and in this way making up on the one part what is lost on the other.

COATS.

The piping on the edges of a Coachman's Frock is put up the fronts, round the collar, round the flaps, sides and bottom, up the opening of back, and across the cuff.

The length of a Coachman's Frock is made to come just above the bend of the knee, say about 36 inch for a 5 feet 8 inch figure.

To remove stains of dirt from Livery overcoats, rub either with a clean piece of the same cloth, a piece of stale bread crumb, or a little French chalk, one or other of these will remove any ordinary soil got on in the ordinary course of making up. If an oil or tar stain gets on, use either benzine or chloroform which are powerful agents in this way.

The Windsor uniform, as worn by Her Majesty's household at Windsor, consists of a blue cloth Evening Dress Coat and scarlet collar and cuffs, three gilt mounted buttons on each side, two at waist, and two on skirt plait. The vest is a Dress Vest and roll collar, and four gilt buttons. Ordinary trousers of blue cloth. White tie. At dinners or evening parties, when uniform is not to be worn, an ordinary black cloth Evening Dress Coat and vest, with trousers of the same material are worn. White tie as usual.

The dress of a British Consul, or a Consul General, is a single breasted coat similar to Diagram 37, made to button up the front with nine gilt buttons, with buttons on hips, and two on the plaits. It is made from blue cloth, with black silk velvet collar and cuffs. Silver embroidery is put on the collar, cuffs, flaps and back, and an embroidered edging of gold on the same parts. Lining of black silk. Breeches of white kersey, with gilt buckle and three covered buttons, and white silk stockings are worn on full dress or state occasions, while trousers of blue cloth, with 2½ inch silver lace laid down the side, are worn for ordinary occasions.

For a Consul the only variation is in the amount of embroidery, which is not brought above the flaps at waist, and the lace is only 1¾ inches wide down the trousers. The cocked hat is also slightly varied. A Vice-Consul's coat is embroidered on collar and cuffs only, and the hat slightly varied, but in other respects it is the same as a Consul's.

For undress, a dark blue cloth double-breasted Frock coat is worn with silk velvet collar and cuffs. Six gilt buttons are placed up each breast, two on hips, and two on pleat. Collar to stand or fall. Slashed cuffs, with three buttons on each. The vest is cut no collar, and made from white, buff or blue. Plain trousers of the same cloth; and the head gear consists of a forage cap with silk lace band, and V.R. embroidered in front and gold embroidered crown.

Consular agents may wear the same uniform as a Vice-Consul during their appointment.

Cancillieris may also wear this, with the exception of plain velvet cuffs to the coat.

Foreign Consuls, Ambassadors, &c., always wear the uniform of the country to which they belong.

The following list of sundries supplied for livery servants will doubtless be useful to our readers, as giving them some idea of the various items enumerated. We may say this list is taken from the price list of a well known retail City trade, whose prices are undoubtedly low.

Hats	10/6, 12/6
Silver Lace Hat Bands, ½ inch wide	4/-
Gold Lace Hat Bands, ½ inch wide	5/-
Black Oakleaf Bands	3/6
Hat Cords, Silver	5/-
Hat Cords, Gold	5/6
Cockades	1/6
Cockades Mourning	3/6
Glazed Hat Covers	3/-
Grooms' Waist Belts	7/6 to 10/6
Driving Gloves	3/- and 3/6
Coachman's Dress Wig	70/- each.
Mourning Aiguilettes	7/6 each.
Mourning Epaulettes	5/- per pair.
Mourning Shoulder Knots	3 - to 4/9
Mourning Gloves	2/9 per pair.
White Berlin Gloves	9d., 10d., 1/- per pair.
Button Stick	6d.
Glove Trees	4/9 and 5/6 per pair.
Jack Trees, for Top Boots	18/6 and 21/- per pair.
Boot Hooks	2/6 and 3/6
Boot Jacks	2/9 and 3/9
Gold and Silver Garters	7/6 to 17/6 per pair.
Stout White Cotton Hose	2/- to 3/- per pair.
Pearl Silk Hose	9/6 to 15/6 per pair.
Black Silk Hose	10/6 to 17/6 per pair.
White Ties	3/6 and 5/6 per dozen.
White Scarfs	9/- per dozen.

(Silver Lace Hat Bands ... Gold Lace Hat Bands) — Advancing 1/- for every additional ¼ inch.

Cockades.

Everyone who has walked much about the West-End of London of late years must have noticed how very much more frequently cockades are worn by servants than formerly.

And if you ask any of your friends who is and who is not entitled to the distinction, you will probably be surprised and amused at the extraordinary diversity of reasons which will be given you for the practice. (There is some little excuse for this, because there is nowhere any authoritative ruling on the subject, and the College of Arms is silent.) The truth is, the matter is entirely one of usage, but has certainly, however, become more or less a social law, and as such well understood in society.

It will therefore be interesting and useful to refer to the origin of the custom. Cockades were first worn in England in the first quarter of the last century. The black cockade, now universally used here, was the Hanoverian badge, and was adopted in contradistinction to the white cockade of the House of Stuart by all officers of the army and navy in the direct service of the Crown; their servants wore them also, to show that though not in uniform they were soldiers and sailors; and, as time went on, the private servants of officers in the two services adopted them. To these may be added all members of the Royal households and the Diplomatic Corps; until comparatively latetimes no one else would have ventured to transgress the bounds of good taste by assuming a distinction to which they had obviously no sort of claim. Thus a rule may be well deduced that none but the servants of those who hold military commissions can have any right.

For example, the servants of Privy Councillors, judges, and magistrates have never worn them; but those of Deputy-

Lieutenants do as holding a quasi-military appointment.

Cockades are of three sorts:

1. The Royal Cockade, which is quite round, and made of flexible leather. This is used only by members of the Royal family, and by some others who claim a Royal descent, such as the Duke of Buccleuch, &c.

2. The Military Cockade. — This is oval, made of stiff leather, and ornamented with a fan or comb. Worn by servants of officers of the army or navy, Lords-Lieutenant, and Deputy-Lieutenants.

3. The Naval or Civil Cockade. — The same as the last, but without the fan. Worn by servants of naval officers, the Diplomatic Corps, and now, by custom, by Ministers of the Crown, and certain high officials, such as the Clerk to the Parliaments, the Black Rod, Serjeant-at-Arms, &c.

It cannot be too clearly understood that a cockade is in no sense a national badge, but simply the mark of a profession.

An attempt has been made to show what are the grounds or foundation upon which the custom rests; but apparently many people consider them merely as a fashionable adjunct to a smart livery — to these this article may be of interest.

It remains to be said, in the light of a recent decision, that for a Parliamentary candidate to pay for the cockades or hat badges of his supporters at an election is a practice bringing a far more speedy and serious penalty than any infraction of the unwritten law of social usage.

COURT DRESS.

THE TRUE ETIQUETTE.

"Dress Worn at His Majesty's Court," edited by Mr. Herbert A. P. Trendell, of the Lord Chamberlain's Department, was published by Messrs. Harrison and Son yesterday. It is beautifully illustrated by Mr. C. E. Collings. The frontispiece is a reproduction of Mr. Archibald Stuart Wortley's portrait of the King in frock dress.

An explanatory memorandum says: "The various widths of embroidery which alone indicate the respective classes to which the wearers are entitled are plainly shown, and ought to settle once and for all many vexed questions.

"The details of the old and new styles of Court dress, either of which can be worn by civilians as preferred, have been carefully set forth, for, owing to want of printed official information, mistakes have constantly been made by wearers of these dresses when attending Court, the particular features of the two styles being erroneously combined. This has been especially noticeable in the case of mayors.

"Special attention is drawn to the waistcoats that should be worn in both styles of velvet Court dress, as these have hitherto been often of wrong material. They should be of white satin or black silk velvet, not of white corded silk or black marcella, these last two materials being only permissible with the cloth Court dress."

Besides the directions for the costume of all classes of subjects at various ceremonials practical hints are given. When in the presence of the Sovereign within the City the Lord Mayor of London wears "the crimson velvet robe of state as for an earl."

MISTAKES OF MAYORS.

The mayoral chain should never be worn with a military uniform, but a mayor who is also a clergyman may attend court in full canonicals, wearing his mayoral chain over his gown. A soft-fronted shirt with white cuffs is the best to wear with uniform. When breeches are worn pants should reach to the knees only, or a combination suit to reach to the knees. With stockings it is advisable to wear a thin pair of cotton hose under the silk. This prevents the flesh being seen through the silk.

Care should be taken to secure swordbelts from showing below coats or waistcoats or above waistcoat openings. This may be achieved by wearing the belt under the braces.

With Court suits plain gold or pearl studs should be in the shirt front, and watch-chains should not be worn. The black silk fob with seal, if worn, should hang from the fob pocket on the right side.

Extract from the Daily Mirror newspaper,
published around 1895.